D0422636

Psycho-feedback

Practical Psychocybernetics

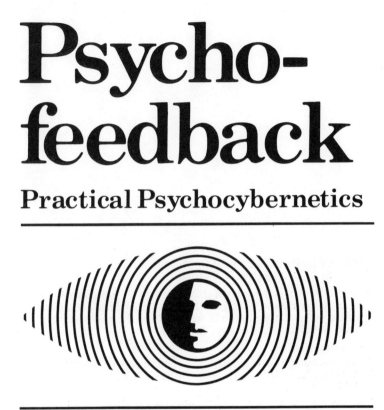

Paul G. Thomas

Publishing History

Psychofeedback was originally published in November 1979
by Prentice-Hall, Inc., Englewood Cliffs, NJ 07632.
ISBN 0-13-732263-1

Prentice-Hall International, Inc., London/Prentice-Hall of
Australia, Pty. Ltd., Sydney/Prentice-Hall of Canada, Ltd., Toronto/
Prentice-Hall of India Private Ltd., New Delhi/Prentice-Hall
of Japan, Inc., Tokyo/Prentice-Hall of Southeast Asia Pte. Ltd.,
Singapore/Whitehall Books Limited, Wellington, New Zealand

The international publishing rights, excluding N. America, were
purchased from Prentice-Hall, Inc. by Psychofeedback Institute,
P.O. Box 49454, Los Angeles, CA 90049, in February 1982.

The N. American publishing rights were purchased from
Prentice-Hall, Inc. by Psychofeedback Institute in August 1982.

20 19 18 17 16 15 14 13 12 11 10 9 8 7

Library of Congress Cataloging in Publication Data
Thomas, Paul G
        Psychofeedback
        1. Success.   2. Feedback (Psychology)   I. Title.
BF637.S8T524   158'.1   79-18695
ISBN 0-9609762-0-5

At the time of going to press with the 7th printing there are Psychofeedback Institute Representatives/Seminar Administrators in over 100 locations in the U.S.A. and Canada.

Grateful acknowledgment is made to the following for permission to reprint from previously published material:

Reprinted by permission from TIME, The Weekly Newsmagazine; copyright Time Inc., 1974.

Rosenblueth, Wiener and Bigelow: "Behaviour, Purpose, and Teleology," *Philosophy of Science.* Copyright 1943, The Williams & Wilkins Co.

Pierre de Latil, *La pensée artificielle.* © Editions Gallimard 1953.

Norbert Wiener, *Cybernetics.* Reprinted by permission of the MIT Press.

John Thurston, review in *The Saturday Review of Literature.*

Excerpts from Wilder Penfield and Lamar Roberts, *Speech and Brain-Mechanisms* (copyright © 1959 by Princeton University Press), pp. 45, 46, 50, 51, 52, and 117. Reprinted by permission of Princeton University Press.

Norbert Wiener, *The Human Use of Human Beings.* Copyright 1950, 1954 by Norbert Wiener. Reprinted by permission of Houghton Mifflin Company.

Two drawings by Dr. Roger W. Sperry, Professor of Psychobiology, California Institute of Technology, from *Neuroscience Third Study Program,* Schmitt and Worden, The MIT Press, 1973.

Dedicated to
the light of my life
my wife
Adita

———————————————————————————

Contents

Introduction

Within the space of a few short years, we have witnessed Yuri Gagarin's trip beyond the pull of earth's gravity; watched Neil Armstrong's giant step for mankind; seen Mariner's landing on Mars, Pioneer's probing the ghastly atmosphere of Venus, and Voyagers I and II taking off on their journey to Jupiter and Saturn. But at the same time, as man was reaching outward from the earth, there were explorations in the opposite direction—into the innermost secrets of life and the mind—that were equally electrifying. One of the most important of these concerned the search for the essential mechanisms of the human brain—the physical bases for all the thoughts, emotions, dreams, inhibitions, motivations, and other psychic characteristics that define who we are and what we may become.

There were many contributing factors which led to

this explosion of knowledge about man's brain and nervous system: the continuing revelations of the electron microscope, which made it possible to examine in the minutest detail the synaptic connections of neurons; the analysis by ultra-centrifugation, which made it possible for us to examine the chemical structure of neurons; the micronization of electronics which made it possible for us to monitor the electrical activity of a single neuron; the discovery that the so-called Autonomic Nervous System had been misnamed and was not beyond the control of the conscious mind; and last, but certainly not least, wonderful techniques of neurosurgery.

Some discoveries in the sixties were so sensational that they easily captured headlines. Wilder Penfield had already surprised the scientific world with his research on electrical stimulation of the brain. This was given a dramatic public demonstration by Jose Delgado who, having implanted electrodes into the brain of a Spanish fighting bull, was able to bring the enraged charging animal to a skidding halt a few feet from the matador whenever a radio signal electrically stimulated its brain.

Roger Sperry's discovery of the different functions of the right and left hemispheres of the brain—a very important discovery in understanding and raising the potential of individuals—did not at first raise quite the excitement as that of his colleague at the California Institute of Technology, James Olds, who located the pleasure centers in the brain. When Olds published his findings, I remember wondering what was the pleasure which could cause his rats to give up food *and* sex just as long as they were able to press the bar which would electrically stimulate their brains. Those rats must have been having a marvelous time, and I'm sure that millions of people wondered about the possibility of having instant happiness or pleasure by command.

James McConnell announced that he had "educated" flatworms to perform particular tasks, that these flatworms had then been eaten up by cannibal flatworms, and that the learning had been transferred to the cannibals. Allen Jacobson announced that he had trained hamsters to enter a feeding box at a particular signal, that he had then killed the hamsters and extracted the chemical RNA from their brains, and that when he had injected the extract into the bloodstream of naïve or untrained rats, they did not require training to respond in the same manner. The experiment said, in effect, that the chemical RNA had actually carried the information "go to feeding-box when you see a light flash" from the hamsters to the rats. Perhaps, people now began to speculate, the secret of learning and memory was at the molecular level and could be manipulated by neurochemists and microbiologists. After all, RNA (ribonucleic acid) is related to DNA (desoxyribose nucleic acid) and it had not been so very much previously that James Watson and Francis Crick had made their monumental discovery of the structure of the DNA molecule, which carries the information of heredity. McConnell's cannibal flatworms prompted one wit to postulate that the way to instant knowledge was to take the brains of professors and teachers, grind them down and inject them into their pupils!

Just as startling was the discovery of the heretofore-unsuspected extent to which we could control our own nervous systems. The word *Biofeedback* did not explode upon us; rather, it was a gradual dawning of the realization that we possess the ability to control many of our internal functions. The public was quick to recognize the significance of the reports which filtered out of the laboratories and clinics, even though they often sounded incredible.

By 1970 public interest was so great that the BBC sent out a production team led by producer Philip Daly and writer Nigel Calder. The result of their investigative trip to eight countries was the P.B.S. program called "The

Mind of Man" which subsequently became a book of the same title by Calder. This was followed by two more books: Maya Pine's *The Brain Changers* and Marilyn Ferguson's *The Brain Revolution,* both published in 1973.

In 1974 both *Time* and *Newsweek* devoted several stories to the subject of brain research. "Inside the Brain" was the cover story of the January 14, 1974, issue of *Time* and, in the limited space available to him, Peter Stoler did a fine job of acquainting the magazine's millions of readers with the exciting developments which were taking place. One of the researchers he interviewed at length was Francis O. Schmitt, then chairman of the M.I.T.-sponsored Neurosciences Research Program and because some of his remarks are in keeping with the content of this book they are worth quoting.

> *Most of our evolution has been somatic. We've changed our shape, but if we could really understand ourselves and by extension each other, we could evolve socially as well. Armies aren't the key to man's survival. Governments are not enough. Treaties are not enough. Only* self-knowledge *will help man to survive.*

Peter Stoler's closing paragraph sets the mood of the time.

> *The ocean that separates man from this self-knowledge remains to be charted. The explorers of the brain have embarked on a journey even more significant than the voyage of Columbus in 1492. Columbus discovered a new continent. The explorers of the brain may well discover a new world.**

Concurrent with the information we were acquiring from

---

*Reprinted by permission from TIME, The Weekly Newsmagazine; copyright Time Inc., 1974.

laboratories about our brain mechanisms was our growing national preoccupation with consciousness. Not only were we beginning to understand that altered states of consciousness could drastically change the ways in which we perceive the world, but also that we have within us incredible powers of self-control and self-fulfillment. Even before biofeedback became a topic of public interest, the conservative American Medical Association had finally conferred respectability on another form of consciousness manipulation. In 1956 the A.M.A. publicly endorsed the use of hypnosis as a useful adjunct to medical practice, a position they should have taken despite Freud's mistaken belief that not everyone can be hypnotized. But from the point of view of the public at large, the origins of the American "consciousness revolution" probably owed far more to the esoteric worlds of Eastern philosophy and the "flower children" than to the sober findings of modern science.

What had been largely confined to the youthful counterculture in the 1960's had mushroomed into something resembling a mass movement by the 1970's. In its September 6, 1976, cover story titled "Getting Your Head Together," *Newsweek* cited an estimate that there were more than 8,000 different consciousness-expanding techniques currently available to the American consumer. Some, such as est, Silva Mind Control and Transcendental Meditation (TM) were skillfully packaged and merchandised, and attracted large, devoted followings and considerable notoriety. Others boldly proclaimed themselves the modern-day successors to classical psychiatry. But all of them had one thing in common: a powerfully attractive promise of individual self-improvement, with all the tangible benefits that flow therefrom: success in work, fulfillment in love, popularity, serenity, strengthened willpower, improved health, and so on and on.

Certainly there is nothing wrong with people wanting such benefits. They are what we all want. We should have to be lamentably arrogant or lazy *not* to want them. But I cannot help wondering how so many people could have imagined that all these various techniques—most of them dissimilar and none of them really tested—could possibly produce the same desirable results.

For instance, the *Newsweek* article tells of one woman who successively tried transactional analysis, primal scream, bioenergetics, yoga, guided fantasy, Arica, lomi body work, nude marathon, gestalt therapy, psychosynthesis and est. And, since the article was written in 1976, there's no telling what she may have been up to since. Plainly this energetic woman wanted to improve herself. But what can her rationale have been? What led her to suppose that *any* of these techniques would be the right one? Perhaps, you may say, there was no way she could have known beforehand which technique was most likely to work. Perhaps she had no choice but to experiment with them all.

I take the point, but I nevertheless disagree with it. I say there *was* a way she could have evaluated the various mind-expansion techniques beforehand—a way vastly more reliable than placing credence in the unsupported claims of the techniques' promoters. By 1976 (and, in fact, well before that) modern scientific research had already provided us with enough proven and tested information about how the human brain functions to permit us not only to know *which* techniques would be most likely to succeed, but also *how* and *why* they would be most likely to succeed.

My guess is that if the woman in the *Newsweek* story had had a little more information about those *hows* and *whys,* she could have come to some fairly accurate conclusions about the merits of the various techniques that were competing for her time and dollars. I think she would have found that most were worthless. that a few—almost inadvertently—did confer some modest benefits, but that, in the end, none fully lived up to its promises because none was based on the understanding of how our brains really operate.

Furthermore, if our *Newsweek* woman had had enough of the then-available scientific information about brain function, and had thought through its implications, she could have created her own self improvement program—one that would have been incomparably better than any of those being offered her by the promoters. It would have been a simple, efficient method, free of intellectual mumbo-jumbo and esoteric claptrap, for giving her an unprecedented degree of control over her thought processes, her moods and emotions, her willpower and her ability to cope successfully with all the people and situations that affected her daily life.

Do you suspect that I am overstating the case? Well, the purpose of this book is to prove to you that I am not. In the pages that follow I intend to explain to you exactly what this method is, how you can use it, and what it will do for you. Most of all, I want to make sure you understand *how* and *why* it works. I want you to be certain that what I am talking about is neither unproven theory nor idle promise, but, instead, is solidly based on scientific fact.

Therefore I shall have to go into a certain amount of detail about both the physical structure of our brains and the cybernetic nature of the ways in which our minds work. If this sounds a little daunting, please do not be alarmed. I think you will find this information as fascinating as it is important, and in the end, I think you will find it both convincing and reassuring.

Moreover—and this is a sad truth—you are not likely to find such information in any other popular books dealing with the subject of consciousness expansion, psychic self-help, or whatever you wish to call it. Even books whose names sound promising—books which use variations of the words *psychic* and *cybernetics* in their titles—more often than not display an appalling ignorance of the very scientific principles and discoveries they seem to be invoking. That is one criticism I hope will never be leveled at this book.

1 What This Book Is About

Whenever I greet a class of new students at one of my Psychofeedback Seminars, I generally begin by asking the group a simple but very important question!

Which would you say is likely to be more important to you, your willpower or your imagination?

Almost invariably, the majority of my students votes for *willpower.* To be sure, my classes are made up largely of hardheaded businessmen and women whom one might expect to place a high value on willpower. But in my experience, most people tend to feel the same way. Because our society has made willpower omnipotent in achieving goals, perhaps you do too.

Nevertheless, the correct answer is—over-whelmingly—*imagination!*

What precisely do I mean by this, and why do I state it so categorically? The answer to the second part of the question is implicit in the first. When I have explained to my students the actual mechanics of the imaginative faculty—when they have tested it and seen for themselves what it can be made to do—they no longer have any doubts about its importance. But of course I do not expect you, at this point, to accept the truth of any of this. My job is to prove it to you. In the pages that follow I will set out all the facts of the matter logically, after which you must judge their validity.

Before I go any further, let me tell you something about myself. I am not a scientist. I am a teacher—one who has adapted and applied the discoveries of great researchers and theoreticians of Cybernetics to the specific needs of his students. To this end I have created a program of instruction that is primarily taught to the executive and sales staffs of public and private corporations. I call my eight-lesson/eight-week course of instruction Psychofeedback Seminars. Although it is mainly taught to salespeople in a number of different industries, it has nothing to do with selling or sales techniques. Nevertheless, the course is specifically intended to, among other things, help professional salespeople achieve the goal of earning more money by increasing their sales. It is a motivational program, yet it is unlike any other program having the same purpose.

Psychofeedback Seminars is based upon three sources of knowledge: the hypotheses and conclusions of the "master cybernetician," Norbert Wiener; the findings of recent research into the mechanics of brain function; and my own emperical knowledge of hypnosis and motivation, which covers a period of twenty years.

How effective is this course of instruction? Let me put it to you in this way. So certain am I that individuals will achieve the high financial goals I ask them to set for themselves, that I have made arrangements with corporations whereby, when their sales staff become my students, I am willing to receive the teaching fee for each individual *only* if his or her sales are increased by an agreed percentage.

At the corporate level, to the best of my knowledge, this arrangement is unique. No other organization I know of is ready to stand or fall on the *results* of its teaching. For me, of course, the practical result of this kind of accountability is all too simple: no results—no money. None of my corporate clients has ever had occasion not to pay my fee for those students who followed through.

Why have I decided to publish the content of my course? Because I believe strongly that the principles of Cybernetics, as they apply to the individual, are so vitally important that it is my duty to attend to a matter which has been neglected for thirty years.

I believe that every person must understand that that part of the brain which functioned at the unconscious level is an information processing mechanism—a biocomputer—within which is a program, and that this program *can* be changed and improved.

I believe that people must understand that they are equipped with a special mechanism whereby they have full access to, and control over, the biocomputer.

I believe that people must also understand that they are able to use a master technique, Psychofeedback, to take them to any goals they set themselves.

All these things have to be learned. But when they *are* learned, for any person who makes sure that the best possible program is in his or her biocomputer, life will take on a quality and pleasure which will be the source of never-ending satisfaction. On the other hand, the person, who refuses to attend to this matter, who refuses to do his duty unto himself, will inevitably fall short of his potential.

I believe that parents and teachers; sales directors

and managers, administrative managers and owners of businesses; athletic directors and coaches—any person in a position to teach or inform others—are duty bound to understand the essentials of psychocybernetics.

Over the past years advertisements have frequently appeared in the press, inserted by individuals or organizations, saying that they are teaching "psychocybernetics." Their modus operandi is invariably the same. They invite the public to a free introductory lecture in a hotel and then prevail upon the audience to sign up for a course of instruction. On three occasions I have attended such lectures and have had my suspicion confirmed: the instructors had no knowledge of the subject. To my way of thinking that is a deplorable state of affairs. It matters not to me who teaches the principles of Cybernetics as they apply to the individual; my concern is that they do so correctly.

I must admit, however, that I do have a purely personal reason for wanting to put the contents of Psychofeedback Seminars between the covers of a book. It is so that my students can have in their hands—in written form—the words which they have heard from me while they have been following my instructions. One of the most important aspects of my program—which is an aspect invariably neglected by other self-improvement programs and is the reason why they have only a short-term effect—is the follow through at the end of the course. An integral part of Psychofeedback Seminars is the use of audio cassettes, which are fifteen minutes in length and which students must use at least once every day. At each lesson students are given a different cassette, the first superseded by the second, the second by the third and so on, until, at the eighth and last lesson they are given the final cassette which they then keep and use on a regular basis.

At the last lesson, I ask every class this question; "Will you allow anything to prevent you from following through?" Then I ask for an answer from each individual in succession. I am sure you can understand that it is very satisfying for me to hear the emphatic "never," "no way," "certainly not," and similar responses which are made by them. It is equally disappointing when I hear of someone not doing so. But the fault is not theirs. Our memories are all too short and unreliable. But from now on there will be no excuse; now my former students will be able to refresh their memories by consulting this book.

All the information contained in this book is exactly what you would have heard in my classes. Obviously there are advantages to being taught by voice in the give-and-take atmosphere of the classroom. However, it is the *transmission* of the information that is the main thing. How the information is received is of no great importance, as long as the information is perceived as being so semantically significant that it will activate the appropriate mechanisms of your mind.

It may interest you to know that it is far easier for me to teach a class than to transmit the same information on paper. Furthermore, in the drafting of the book, in arranging the sequence of the information, it has become obvious to me that I am going to have to use such expressions as, "we will come back to this matter in a later chapter" or "as you will see presently." Anywhere I do that you can be sure it is better for you that we do not digress from the matter under discussion. It will only be done to ensure that the conceptual thread of information, fragile at the best of times, is not broken. In a class, there is a teaching technique whereby I can repeat information without being tedious and yet not break the conceptual thread.

I mention these "transmission" difficulties because prior to concluding publishing arrangements with Prentice-Hall, Inc., I had an experience which astonished me. When I had written a rough draft of this book, I decided to contact some publishers. Two of them, both well known as publishers of self-improvement books, returned the manuscript with these comments: from the first, that "the subject is too highbrow" and from the second, that "it is too scientific." The implication of these comments, assuming that publishers judge a book on the potential of sales created by public demand, is that, in their view, the public is so slow-witted that it can only be satisfied by platitudes and simplifications.

I just cannot believe that. My experience has been that the vast majority of Americans are intelligent, open-minded and, providing they have reasonable proof of the validity of a concept which does not conflict with any deeply held beliefs, have the flexibility to accept and act vigorously upon the concept, if they think it will improve their circumstance in life.

Ironically it is true that the more successful an individual is, the greater his or her alacrity to learn about Cybernetics, Psychofeedback, and the rest. It is ironic, because that person is intuitively doing some of the things which I teach. What he gets from me is a refinement, a sharpening of his faculties.

As to "beliefs," nowhere in this book will you find anything which will clash with your chosen religious persuasion for the simple reason that I do not presume to invoke the name of God or level admonitions at you. And I certainly do not intend to insult you. For Werner Erhard's est people to kick Bibles across the stage and describe religion as "bullshit," which, according to the Los Angeles *Times,* of July 16, 1978, they did in the town of Salinas, California, is, simply, outrageous. I hope you never have the misfortune of such an experience. Incidentally, I might mention that the est program can have a demotivating effect because stoic resignation to "what is, is" is not compatible with the demands of our society.

Past students may notice that some of the information which was not authenticated by me in class is done so herein. While the student in class is told all that you will be reading, I do not expect my statements about neurophysiology to have to be supported and confirmed by the eminent authorities whose words you will be reading.

One of the disadvantages of having my program in book form is that I will not be able to stop you from getting ahead of me in assimilating and processing the information. Words such as "psychofeedback" and "Rascon" are perhaps unfamiliar to you so your curiosity may get the better of you and you may want to turn immediately to the chapters dealing with these two mind mechanisms. Please do not. If you do, you may get confused. I have tried to sequence the information so that you will have no difficulty in understanding the fundamentals of your own brain mechanisms. I would like you to read the book in its entirety and, along the way, to do those things which I ask you to do. It is important that you try to observe these rules if the words which you read are to be meaningful to you.

One final word about the assumptions on which this book is based. At the corporate level, there is a mistaken idea that people can *be* motivated. You cannot motivate people. The manager who thinks that his actions motivate people is ignoring the fact that motivation is essentially a personal matter. It is a problem of the mind/brain mechanisms of the individual, and because this is so, individual responsibility must remain absolute—particularly in a power evolving cybernetic society like our own that places such a heavy emphasis on competition for success.

In this connection I should point out that one of the odd by-products of our society's preoccupation with success is that it sometimes has the effect of *inhibiting* motivation. Some people persist in believing that anything short of what society defines as success is failure. As a result, considering themselves failures, they give up trying.

This, of course, is the worst kind of folly. We should never view our lives in terms of failure, but only in terms of *degrees of success.* Even the "least successful" people are, in some respects, great successes. The Skid Row drunk may be reckoned one of the greatest failures in our society, but at what he wants to do—get booze—he can be eminently successful, often pursuing his goal with an ingenuity that you or I would be hard put to match. There will be people who will say that there is a difference between addiction and habit. Perhaps they are right. But even they have to admit that the program in the biocomputer of the derelict—"get booze by any means"—never lets him down. Whether his goal is a good one, or is worth pursuing, is a matter not of success, but of values. The point is that you can use the same mechanism to accomplish whatever goals you set for yourself.

And even when values are shared, when people are competing for the same goal, the "either-or" distinction between success and failure is never valid. The person who earns $10,000 a year may be less successful than the person earning $100,000. *But only less successful: Not a failure!* And since none of us ever really attains all his possible goals, we are all alike in that we represent *degrees of success.*

At the corporate level the most a manager can and should do is to help people become more motivated by guiding them to the source of their own power. At the personal level, the age-old question has been, "How can I become *permanently* motivated to do those things I know I have to do if I want to be more successful, and yet still enjoy the pleasures that surround me?"

But what is motivation exactly? I define it as follows:

> *Motivation is the energizing and control of purposeful behavior toward specific goals.*

Contained within this definition are two concepts of crucial importance: *goals* and *control*. But what I mean by these concepts may not be precisely what you think I mean, for I am using them in their cybernetic sense. In order to make things clearer, I am now going to ask you to become better acquainted with the astonishing world of Cybernetics and the work of its founding genius, Norbert Wiener.

2 Cybernetics and the Genius of Norbert Wiener

It can be said that the gestation period of Cybernetics, from the germination of the idea to the birth of the concept, was approximately ten years in the decade prior to 1947.

In the 1930's, Arturo Rosenblueth, then professor at Harvard Medical School, organized and led monthly dinner meetings at Vanderbilt Hall. The group consisted of men from different fields of endeavor drawn from the various faculties of Harvard University. After dinner, one of the guests would read a paper on some scientific topic, generally one in which questions of methodology were the main consideration. The speaker then had to run the gauntlet of good-natured but unsparing criticism from the group.

Doubtless, Rosenblueth's original purpose in organizing these meetings was for the exchange of ideas and for the entertainment of stimulating conversation.

Then something happened which, in retrospect, undoubtedly affected the lives of an uncountable number of men and women.

Introduced to these monthly dinner meetings, first as an invited guest and then as a regular member, came Norbert Wiener, a professor of mathematics at the Massachusetts Institute of Technology. If I have a regret in my life, it is that I never met or heard this intellectual giant of the twentieth century.

Out of those lively discussions came the notion that perhaps the men of medicine, of physics, of mathematics and of engineering had limited themselves intellectually by conforming too closely to the rigidities of specialization. Men working in different fields of specialization were having increasing difficulty in communicating with one another. Often the concepts they worked with, and even the language they used, could not be understood outside the narrow confines of their own disciplines. Could this very rigidity be delaying the advancement of science? Was it possible that the man who took pulse and temperature needed to find some common ground for understanding the man adept at operating a cyclotron?

Norbert Wiener was the catalyst; the common denominator was mathematics. Wiener was able to show that modern mathematics was not only concerned with quantities, figures, and values, but that the *quality* of things could be shown mathematically, as well.

Fortunately, a deep and close relationship developed between Rosenblueth and Wiener. Both men were committed to the advancement of science. Both were convinced that the most fruitful areas for the growth of the sciences were those which had been neglected as a no-man's land between the various established disciplines.

The physician and the mathematician insisted that a proper exploration of "these blank spaces on the map of science" could be made only by a team of scientists, each a specialist in his own field, but each possessing a sound acquaintance with the field of his neighbors. All team members would be in the habit of working together and of knowing one another's intellectual habits. The mathematician, for example, would not need to have the skill to conduct a physiological experiment, but he should have the skill to understand one, to criticize one, and even to suggest one.

The two men dreamed for years of an institution of independent scientists working together, joined by the desire to understand science as a whole and to lend one another the strength of that understanding. As happened in many other fields, World War II was to help turn this dream into a reality.

In the summer of 1940, Wiener turned his attention to the development of digital computers and to the investigation of how the control of antiaircraft guns could be improved upon.

Working with another mathematician, Julian Bigelow, on the second project, Wiener realized that a very important factor involved in improving the performance of gunner and gun against pilot and plane was what control engineers call Feedback. This led Wiener to a complete investigation of feedback techniques and under what circumstances or conditions feedback mechanisms could go out of kilter and break down.

It is in the conclusions that Wiener drew from this investigation that we are able to appreciate his towering intellect and the prodigious breadth of his mind. I wonder who else could have examined the way the steering mechanism of a ship can go into ever-increasing oscillation and eventually break down, and then compare this with the inability of a human being suffering from Purpose Tremor in reaching out to pick up an object, and identify in both phenomena a common principle: that the cause of both defects was due to excessive Feedback.

The concept involved in these notions was so different from the view then current among neurophysiologists (which was that the brain sent signals outward to muscles and there the process stopped) that it was left to the physician, Rosenblueth, to disseminate the information to his own profession at a meeting of physicians in New York in 1942, organized under the auspices of the Josiah Macy Foundation.

In 1943 Rosenblueth, Wiener, and Bigelow distilled the content of their ideas in a paper titled "Behavior, Purpose and Teleology" (for "Teleology" read "Feedback") which was published in the journal *Philosophy of Science*.*

Because "Behavior, Purpose and Teleology" is such an important document and because contained within it we see the indispensability of Feedback to all purposeful activity, so that it might have a wider readership, I have purchased a license to republish it in its entirety at the end of this book, as an appendix. Interestingly, only once in this article does a word appear which was to be one of the foundation stones of the new ideas. The word is *Information*.

Although the word Cybernetics was not coined until 1947, it will be better for you if I now stop using such words as "ideas" and "notions" and use the word Cybernetics instead. We will get to the origin and derivation of Cybernetics in a moment.

By now men from another fledgling science were also showing interest in Cybernetics. These scientists were developing computers. In time their involvement with Cybernetics would prove crucial. Their work was to be another foundation stone of Cybernetics.

By 1944 so many scientists from so many separate disciplines were showing an interest in Cybernetics that

---

*Rosenblueth, Wiener and Bigelow: "Behavior, Purpose and Teleology," *Philosophy of Science*. Copyright 1943, The Williams & Wilkins Co.

Wiener and John von Neumann, a mathematician at Princeton's Institute of Advanced Studies, arranged a symposium at Princeton University. Other meetings followed, and soon the fame of the emerging new science had spread to scientific circles in Western Europe and South America. By 1947 it was time for Cybernetics to be introduced to the general public.

Since I happen to consider Wiener's decision to share his ideas with the world at large one of the landmarks of modern civilization, I hope you will forgive me if I pause to tell you the story in some detail. Among other things, the anecdote illustrates the almost accidental ways in which monumental things are sometimes accomplished.

What happened was this: In the spring of 1947 Wiener stopped off in Paris on his way back from a mathematics conference in Nancy. There he met M. Freymann, director of the French scientific publishing firm of Hermann et Cie. Freymann and Wiener seemed to hit it off from the start, and before long, according to their mutual friend, Pierre de Latil, the following conversation took place:

> *"Why don't you write a book on the theories that you are always talking about?"*
>
> *"The public isn't ripe yet.* Maybe in another twenty years . . ."*
>
> *"All the same, I think I know of a publisher who might be interested. . . ."*
>
> *"No publisher would ever take such a risk!"*
>
> *"Oh, I think he might."*
>
> *The interchange continued thus for a moment, and then Wiener suddenly said, "I get you! You are the publisher." They shook hands on it. "In three months' time I shall hand over my manuscript." But when Wiener left, Freymann smiled and said, "Of course he'll never give it another thought"; and in fact, no further mention was made of the subject*

throughout Wiener's stay in Paris.

Three months later, however, an air-mail package arrived at the Rue de la Sorbonne. Freymann opened it—and there was the manuscript. A quarter of an hour later one of the printers working for Hermann et Cie came to seek orders for work, or men would have to be "laid off" the next day. "There's something to get on with—that manuscript on the table over there."

So, eleven days later, since there was no other work on hand, the type was already set and the proofs dispatched to America by air. An acknowledging cable arrived: You'll have to beat American efficiency twice over. A call then came from Boston, from the Director of Technology Press, the publications organ of the M.I.T., asking Freymann to release Wiener from his contract: the M.I.T. could not let the work of one of its own professors be published by another firm.

"Only Wiener himself can ask to be released from his contract," was Freymann's reply. "Besides, the type is already set." Some days later the M.I.T. offered to reimburse the publisher's expenses. After six telephone calls they reached an agreement. So as not to place Wiener in a difficult position vis-a-vis his University, Freymann agreed to publish his work in collaboration with the Technology Press, but he retained sole copyright for all countries and it was the Paris edition that was universally distributed. This is how a French publisher came to publish a book in English that has sold throughout the world. The story is worth recounting, above all for its ending: the book sold twenty-one thousand copies!*

---

*From *La pensée artificiellie*, Pierre de Latil, © Editions Gallimard 1953.

Subsequently, M.I.T. purchased the copyright from Hermann et Cie and there have been many printings, both of the M.I.T. and John Wiley editions. It is this book which, as I hope to show you, contains some of the great secrets of all human endeavor.

Between the time of making the arrangement with Freymann and completing the manuscript, Wiener had to choose a name for the subject matter. Here is how he described the process:

> *We were seriously hampered by the lack of unity of the literature concerning these problems, and by the absence of any common terminology, or even a single name for the field. We have come to the conclusion that all the existing terminology has too heavy a bias to one side or another to serve the future development of the field as well as it should. We have been forced to coin at least one neo-Greek expression to fill the gap. We have decided to call the entire field of control and communication theory, whether in the machine or in the animal, by the name of Cybernetics, which we form from the Greek χυβερνήτης kubernetes or steersman.*

In the subtitle of his book, Wiener attempted to define the new term:

Cybernetics
or
Control and Communication
in the Animal and the Machine

What Wiener was trying to say in the subtitle was that he had chosen the word Cybernetics to describe the comparative study which has been made into the way in which machines, in particular computers, work and the way in which the brain and body of animals work. Psychocybernetics has the same definition, except the end must read, "brain, body *and* human mind work."

One of my heroes, Sir Winston Churchill, once said, "All the great things are simple, and many can be expressed in a single word: freedom; justice; honor; duty; mercy; hope." Similarly, Wiener intended the word Cybernetics to be all-embracing. In his search for a word, what did he say? "All the existing terminology has too heavy a bias [either] to one side [i.e., machines or artificial systems], or to another [i.e., animals or natural systems]." Unfortunately, what Wiener was trying to avoid did happen: the conceptual interpretation has moved steadily and increasingly toward an association with artificial systems.

Perhaps the reason for the conceptual drift away from the true meaning of Cybernetics as Wiener intended it is because it was so new. It is easy to conceptualize words such as Churchill used—"justice," "duty," etc.— but with something as new as this, those people who studied Wiener's work inevitably arrived at their own interpretations.

Even so, the sheer importance of Wiener's book was not lost on most thoughtful people. John Thurston, who reviewed *Cybernetics* in *The Saturday Review of Literature,* wrote:

> *It appears impossible for anyone seriously interested in our civilization to ignore this book. It is a "must" book for those in every branch of science. In addition, economists, politicians, statesman and business men cannot afford to overlook cybernetics and its tremendous implications.*

And Isaac Asimov said:

> *Cybernetics is not merely another branch of science. It is an Intellectual Revolution which rivals in importance the earlier Industrial Revolution.*

Nevertheless, it seems to me that Cybernetics has still not yet fulfilled its promise, and that, on the thirtieth anniversary of Wiener's book, a redefining of the word may help to correct the conceptual imbalance. I suggest the following:

> *Cybernetics is the word used to describe the study of comparisons made between all self-organizing systems, information-processing systems, and the related methods of controlling such systems.*

The word *all* is to be taken literally: it applies to commerce, sociology, politics, psychology, and the individual. A political party is a self-organizing system. A corporation is a self-organizing system. Every human being is a self-organizing system.

As to the individual, Plato puts the words in the voice of Socrates as a substantive, with the meaning of "science of navigation." In a dialogue with Callicles on character, Socrates says, "Cybernetics saves men's lives, bodies and material possessions from the gravest perils."

Many years later, in the early 1800's, the French physicist André-Marie Ampère used the word again, this time a little differently. According to Ampère, "cybernetics" was the word that should be given to that branch of politics that is concerned with government. If he had specified *self-government,* he might not have been too far from Wiener's definition.

In the years since Wiener wrote *Cybernetics,* many people have tenaciously persisted in the error of thinking that the word applies solely to machines, and especially to computers. One person who tried to correct this misimpression—at least as far as lay readers were concerned—was plastic surgeon Maxwell Maltz. In his popular 1960 book, *Psycho-Cybernetics,* Maltz wrote:

> *When we conceive of the human brain and nervous system as a form of servo-mechanism operating in*

> *accordance with Cybernetic principles, we gain a*
> *new insight into the why and wherefore of human*
> *behavior. I choose to call this new concept*
> *"Psycho-Cybernetics." . . .*

Of course, "new" was just what the concept was not. Maltz's only contribution was a new name; Wiener had intended this concept all along. Nevertheless, Maltz performed a useful service in acquainting his readers with the fact that the principles of Cybernetics could be applied just as appropriately to the functions of the human brain as to the operations of sophisticated machines. He understood—almost intuitively, it seems—that embodied in the concepts of Cybernetics were keys that could unlock the doors to achievement for every human being.

Yet, disappointingly, Maltz did not really follow up on this important insight. His book shows some understanding (though, in my opinion, not nearly enough) of basic Feedback principles, but by today's standards, it seems woefully uninformed both about brains and about machines. Maltz cannot be blamed for this. After all, in 1960 the computer revolution—made possible by the invention of the transistor and the consequent development of miniaturization and integrated circuits—was just beginning. Maltz was in the awkward position of a man who has made an important discovery but cannot explain how it works.

Well then, how *does* it work? In what ways do our brains function like computers, and our computers function like brains? And what vital lessons can we learn from these comparisons? These are the matters to which we must turn now.

3 Computers and Biocomputers

All computers are capable of very rapidly performing complex calculations. They can compile, correlate, and select data, and generally solve difficult problems by virtue of:

(1) Having an Input and an Output;
(2) Having stored information and instructions. The instructions are called the program.

Input refers to information that is inserted or taken into the machine. This information is converted into a code—a binary arithmetic code. The coded information is processed and acted upon by the machine, in accordance with instructions and other information (the program) also stored in the same code. When the machine has completed its assignment, it decodes the answer back into the language of the user, and either prints the answer on paper or displays it on a screen. This is what is known as Output.

The words "taken into" require some further explanation.

We are all becoming very familiar with symbols such as these on groceries we buy in the market. I doubt if you can find a packaged item in your kitchen which you have recently purchased without these symbols. Even magazines have them. This particular set of symbols is from the magazine *New West*. They mean nothing to us, but the  computer can "read" them with a photoelectric "eye." In this sense, the information is not so much deliberately inserted into the machine as "taken in" by the machine itself.

Perhaps you are wondering why I have not used the word *memory* in the description I have given above. I have excluded it deliberately. Properly speaking, memory is a human function. To use the word in connection with machines is a throw-back to the days of "giant brains," artifacts from the imagination of science-fiction writers. Although the term was adopted by some computer scientists, it would have been better if they had not done so, because to most people the word *memory* means *recall*. If people say they have poor memories, they mean they have difficulty remembering and recalling. Computers, of course, never have that problem.

But if human memory is not always as reliable as a computer's ability to retrieve stored information, the analogy is still very close. It is especially close, with regard to Input, Output, and Programs. Input comes into our brains in the form of all sorts of information, from raw data provided by our senses to elaborately structured ideas presented to us by ourselves and other people. We process this information through a variety of Programs we carry within us, from simple reflex arcs to sophisticated codes of thought and behavior we have learned from a lifetime of experience. The result of this processing is our Output: actions we take, conclusions we draw, emotions we feel.

There is another essential element of computer performance which Wiener realized made the comparisons between computer and brain even more significant. Since the 1940's, when digital computers made their first appearance, *speed* of operation has been a high priority of the engineers and manufacturers; but this desire has always had to be tempered by the necessity of *accuracy* and *reliability*. Obviously, the same factors apply to human action. In the case of computers, Wiener pointed out:

> . . . *a chain of operations, each covering a fraction of a millisecond, may last a matter of hours or days. It is quite possible for a chain of computational operations to involve 10^{10} separate steps. Under these circumstances, the chance that at least one operation will go amiss is very far from negligible. . . .*
>
> *[The best] method of checking, and in fact the one generally used in practice, is to refer every operation simultaneously to two or three separate mechanisms. If three separate mechanisms are used for each stage, and single misfunctions are as rare as they are in fact, there will practically always be an agreement between two of the three mechanisms, and this agreement will give the required result. In this case, the collation mechanism accepts the majority report, and the machine need not stop; but there is a signal indicating where and how the minority report differs from the majority report. If this occurs at the first moment of discrepancy, the indication of the position of the error may be very precise.*

Interrupting Wiener's line of reasoning for a moment, I would like you to remember: that he wrote the above in 1947, when computers were constructed from electronic tubes, mechanical relays, resistors and capacitors. For instance the ENIAC machine of that era was made from nearly half a million parts, of which over 18,800 were electronic tubes. The chances that ENIAC would make a mistake were much greater than for today's computers. Nevertheless, depending on the importance of the function being carried out by the system, exactly the same method as Wiener described is used today. For instance, where human life is involved, as it is on modern passenger-carrying aircraft which have computerized inertial-guidance systems, there are always three separate computers. One of them does the work while the second monitors everything the first is doing; the third stands by and is activated only if there is a disagreement between the other two. The chances of a disagreement between one and two expressed as odds against are statistically staggering, but should one occur, the majority report would be accepted. Where the defense of the country is concerned, I understand it is usual to have as many as twelve separate systems monitoring each other, which is a comforting thought! But let us return to Wiener as he compares the computer and the brain:

> *It is conceivable and not implausible that at least two of the elements of this process are also represented in the [human] nervous system. We can hardly expect that any important message is entrusted for transmission to a single neuron, or that any important operation is entrusted to a single neuronal mechanism. Like the computing machine, the brain probably works on a variant of the famous principle expounded by Lewis Carroll in* The Hunting of the Snark: *"What I tell you three times is true."*

What Wiener described as "conceivable and not implausible," is exactly how the brain functions.

Thus, human beings may truly be said to have the same general characteristics as computers. They have Input and Output, stored information and instructions, and also, to ensure some measure of reliability, three mechanisms which are used essentially for cross-checking and comparing. Marvelously integrated, these are, in fact, storage mechanisms, which are, in the order I will explain them to you, Experiential Storage, Word Storage, and Conceptual Storage. I will say much about these three mechanisms a little later on, but first let us take a brief look at our "hardware"; the actual flesh-and-blood machine we call our brain.

The human brain is remarkably compact. It weighs only about 50 ounces in the average adult male and about 5 ounces less in the average woman. It requires only about 1/10 volt of electricity to perform efficiently, yet it is composed of literally tens of billions of nerve cells. Although the brain operates both less rapidly and less accurately than a computer, it leaves even the most advanced computer far behind in its truly staggering *capacity*. The network of interconnections (called *synapses*) between the billions of nerve cells (*neurons*) in the brain is potentially able to process information bits in ways whose number is equivalent to 2 to the 10^{13}. This is a number considerably greater than the total of all the atoms in the entire universe! Yet so neatly packaged is the human brain that in order even to approach such a capacity, a modern computer would have to be at least *10,000 times larger* than the average brain.

Much of this enormous capacity goes unused. Even granting that, at best, we process information more slowly than computers, the average rate at which we process is probably less than 2 percent the rate we can achieve when we are concentrating and thinking hard. Can you imagine what mental prodigies we should all be if we could improve our average rate of processing from 2 percent to, say, 4 percent of our potential?

Nevertheless, the evolution of the human brain seems consistently to have emphasized overall capacity above speed and accuracy. Perhaps the answer lies in the tremendous survival value of our highly developed "memories"—our ability to store away not only huge quantities of information but also a vast array of programs through which we can process this information in specifically useful ways. When Hamlet says, "What a piece of work is man! how noble in reason! how infinite in faculty!" Shakespeare was writing something not far from literal truth. If by "faculty" Shakespeare had been referring to the number of possible ways in which each of us can use the approximately 250 billion bits of information we process during a lifetime, the number really would seem to approach infinity!

The map of the brain can be divided into three main zones arranged rather like the layers of an onion. At the center, connected to the top of the spinal column, is the brain stem. Surrounding this is the limbic system; and surrounding that, the cortex. Attached to the lower back of the "onion" is a fourth zone,—the cerebellum,—but this does not seem to be involved in cognitive functions, as the other three are.

It once was thought that only the cortex was concerned with the conscious thought processes, and that specific areas of the cortex were associated with specific classes of thought. It is apparent now that any such description would be a gross oversimplification. The fact is that all parts of the brain are intricately interconnected. The brain is, of course, the seat of the mind.

It has become customary to refer to the mind as being in two parts: conscious mind and "sub-conscious mind." This, of course, is quite incorrect. You do not have, in fact, you cannot have a "sub-conscious mind." You have a mind. Period. And modern science has even pinpointed its exact location. This is a small part of our brain, probably no more than 1 percent of the total, situated in the higher brain stem in the central gray matter and part of the reticular formation, which can be called the physical basis of the mind.

It was discovered by two distinguished physiologists, Drs. H. W. Magaun and G. Moruzzi, who gave it the name Reticular Activating System—RAS. You can read an account of their research in *The Waking Brain* by H. W. Magaun.

The RAS is about four inches long and about as thick as a man's little finger. Its exact location is shown in Figure 1. It is the *only* part of the brain that connects with every other part of the brain and the rest of the body. It is the *only* part of the brain that ceases all activity whenever we lose consciousness, whatever the reason—violence, anaesthetic, illness or merely going to sleep. Writing in the *Scientific American* in May 1957, about ten years after the RAS was discovered by Magaun and Moruzzi, Dr. John French commented: "The RAS underlies our awareness of the world and our ability to think, to learn and to act. Without it, an individual is reduced to a helpless, senseless, paralyzed blob of protoplasm."

If we equate the mind with consciousness, there can be no doubt that the RAS is the physical basis of the mind.

I realize this will seem strange to you and that there may be a tendency on your part to doubt this because the "sensation" of the result of the activities of the mind seem to be located behind our forehead. But a similar phenomenon occurs with our vision. The "sensation" of seeing seems to be in our eyes, and yet our eyes are only the receptors of visual information. The processing of this information goes on at the back of our head in our visual cortex, but we have no "sensation" of seeing in that location.

I am most grateful to Dr. W. Jann Brown, professor

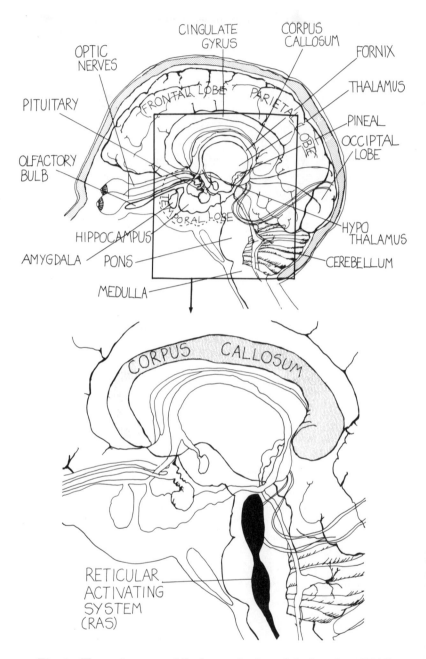

Fig. 1 The major areas of the human brain and the location of RAS

of pathology and psychiatry, University of California at Los Angeles Medical School, for spending a Saturday morning with me, giving me a lesson in neuroanatomy— even going to the extent of dissecting a brain so that I might see for myself the RAS, this physical base of consciousness and the mind.

But what is the work of this small part of the brain and what is its relationship to the rest of the brain? Can the functions of the RAS, the mind, be clearly defined? Perhaps not in every respect, but in the ways that constitute the major point of this book they most certainly can!

Before I enumerate the three crucial functions of the RAS, I want to be sure that you understand how I am using one of the words in my description. The English language is rich in anomaly, in words having three, four, and more meanings and perhaps as many more connotations for each. These shades of meaning give English its beauty, but from a communcations point of view they can be its downfall.

The word is *environment.*

Say "environment" to most people, and because of its most common usage, it immediately triggers thoughts of green fields, trees, and pollution. When I use the word *environment,* I mean *whatever it is that you are doing and wherever you are at any given moment of the day.* At the moment that you are reading this, the place that you are in is your environment, and the people who are with you in the place—if there are any—are all part of your environment. Even the words on this page are part of your environment.

Now, back to the RAS. The three separate duties or functions of the RAS are

> *(1) To take cognizance of your environment, to be analytical, to be critical, to accept or reject conditions of your environment and to activate thoughts relative to the conditions of your en-*

> *vironment. (I have emphasized* reject *for a par-*
> *ticular reason, and will explain shortly.)*

The other two functions which the RAS must perform—
and I am putting these *in order of their importance*—are

> *(2) To activate the mechanism of your imagina-*
> *tion*
> *(3) To activate the mechanism of your willpower.*

I do not want to give you the impression that the RAS is
so important that all the other parts of the brain must
take second place. All the parts of the brain are elaborately interconnected. Isolated from the cortex, the limbic system, and the rest, the RAS would be a poor thing
indeed. Whenever I speak of specific functions of the
RAS, I always mean the RAS *in active collaboration with
all other brain functions.*

From what I have said about the RAS so far, it is
clear that one of the important brain functions with
which the RAS must interact is "memory"—or, if you will
permit me to use the more accurate language of Cybernetics, information storage.

Obviously, information storage has to take place at
the unconscious level. If at every waking moment we
were simultaneously aware of all the billions of bits of
information stored in the memory circuits of our brains,
we should quickly go mad.

To get a picture of what those parts of the brain
which function at the unconscious level do, we must turn
to the work of a brilliant researcher, Dr. Wilder Penfield.
Neurosurgeon, scientist, explorer, and writer, he was for
many years before his retirement director of the Mon-
treal Neurological Institute and professor of neurology
and neurosurgery at McGill University. A number of
books and papers were written by Penfield and co-
authored with his colleagues about their work. One book

in particular brings the entire concept of Cybernetics sharply into focus, and makes the logic of "the comparative study" irrefutable. The book is *Speech and Brain-Mechanisms,* co-authored by Drs. Wilder Penfield and Lamar Roberts. (It is from this book that the quotations given below are taken.*)

Some of Penfield's most illuminating work concerns information storage. Even though some functions are controlled by fairly well defined areas of the brain, there is one human function which does not have a very well defined area, and that is the speech and vocalization mechanism. (In fact, the motor, auditory, and visual centers are also involved in this mechanism.) When neurosurgery is necessary, it is a primary concern of the surgeon that he can operate without impairing the ability to speak. This is particularly so in the case of removal of lesions caused by epileptic seizures.

The technique, pioneered by Wilder Penfield, of ensuring a minimum impairment of the speech mechanism, is to stimulate the brain electrically while the patient is speaking. The patient is shown objects, or pictures of objects, and he is asked to identify and name the object. He does not know if and when the brain is being stimulated. Whenever the brain is stimulated the surgeon drops a small piece of paper on the spot on the head where the stimulus was applied. The paper has on it an identifying number, which then acts as the key of the response which was elicited.

It was as long ago as 1933 (although he did not publish his findings until the 50's) that Penfield made the startling discovery that when the brain of a certain patient was electrically stimulated, she relived an experi-

---

*Excerpts from Wilder Penfield and Lamar Roberts, *Speech and Brain-Mechanisms* (copyright © 1959 by Princeton University Press), pp. 45, 46, 50, 51, 52, and 117. Reprinted by permission of Princeton University Press.

ence which she had had earlier in her life. This discovery set Penfield off on a voyage of exploration of the human brain. Since that time many patients have agreed to cooperate and have their brains probed and electrically stimulated.

The following are some of the accounts, together with Penfield's observations:

> *A young man, JT, who had recently come from his home in South Africa, cried out when the superior surface of his right temporal lobe was being stimulated: "Yes, Doctor! Now I hear people laughing—my friends—in South Africa." After stimulation was over, he could discuss his double awareness and express his astonishment, for it had seemed to him that he was with his cousins at their home where he and the two young ladies were laughing together. He did not remember what they were laughing at. Doubtless he would have discovered that also, if the strip of experience had begun earlier, or if the surgeon had continued the stimulation a little longer. This was an experience from his earlier life. It had faded from his recollective memory, but the ganglionic pattern which must have been formed during that experience was still intact and available to the stimulating electrode. It was at least as clear to him as it would have been had he closed his eyes and ears thirty seconds after the event and rehearsed the whole scene "from memory." Light and sound and personal interpretation—all were recreated for him by the electrode.*

In the case of MMa, Penfield wrote:

> *. . . when an electrode, insulated except at the tip, was introduced through a point one centimeter into*

the cortex of the superior surface of the temporal lobe and a gentle current was switched on, she exclaimed: "Oh, a familiar memory—in an office somewhere. I could see the desks. I was there and someone was calling to me—a man leaning on a desk with a pencil in his hand." All the details of those things to which she had paid attention in some previous period of time were still there. Perhaps the pencil in his hand had seemed important, but other images that must have reached her retina during the original experience are now lost, probably because they were ignored originally.

The comment in the preceding paragraph about the pencil, by Penfield, will become clearer to you later, when we discuss storage relative to its durability.

Penfield concludes:

The patients have never looked upon an experiential response as a remembering. Instead of that it is a hearing-again and seeing-again, a living through moments of past time.

I would not think that you have any doubt remaining that every experience that every individual has ever had is stored in the unconscious. This then is the first of the three basic kinds of storage: EXPERIENTIAL STORAGE.

Sometimes an electrode can completely inhibit the neurons concerned with a particular word. Returning to *Speech and Brain-Mechanism* again, when patient CH had his brain stimulated at point 26, and at the same time was shown a picture of a human foot, this is what happened:

26—The patient said, "Oh, I know what it is. That is what you put in your shoes." After withdrawal of

the electrode he said "foot."
27—Unable to name "tree" which was being shown
to him. Instead he said, "I know what it is." Elec-
trode was withdrawn then and he said "tree."

At both points CH knew what it was that he was looking at *but could not say* the word, "foot" or "tree."

From experiments such as this we have learned that for every word in our vocabulary there are groups of neurons which are only concerned with that word.

This is the second kind of storage: WORD STORAGE. Now to the third kind of storage.

When CH looked at the picture of a foot, and the word "foot" was blocked by the stimulating electrode, what did he say? He said, "I know what it is. That is what you put in your shoes." When he said that, he certainly was not referring to his hand or his stomach. Something "you put in your shoes" is a concept of a foot, If you had been in the position of CH, you might have chosen another concept, you might have said, "That's the thing which has toes on it." I might have said, particularly if I had any, "I have corns on it." All are concepts of a foot.

Another example: I'm thinking of a word, but I am not going to tell you what the word is for the moment. I am going to conceptualize it. This word describes an insect, a very colorful and fragile insect. It has a wide wing span, and it flies in the spring and summer. It comes from a caterpiller and a chrysalis. It is not a moth but that is close. Now, if by this time you are not thinking "butterfly," either I am a poor conceptualizer or you are a poor imaginer. All of the above, of course, are concepts of a "butterfly," and so we come to the third kind of storage: CONCEPTUAL STORAGE.

Now let me give you an example of how the integration of the three storage mechanisms ensure a measure of reliability. In a moment, I am going to write a word. When you have read the word, I want you to look away from the page for a few seconds—say five or six seconds—as you try to recognize this word. The word is "nomel." Now look away from the page and think.

While you had your eyes away from the page, you were searching, scanning your word storage. If you do crossword puzzles, you may have recognized the word immediately. If you don't and are continuing to search your word storage, you are getting a "not known," a "no go" signal.

The word "nomel" is actually another word spelled backwards. Look at it again. Now what has happened? Immediately, given the correct information, you found the word in your word storage and you received a "recognized go" signal. Immediately, also, a number of concepts were tossed up into your mind. You might be thinking of the sharp taste or the pungent smell or the yellow color of a "nomel" spelled in the conventional way.

As we have seen, in those parts of your brain which function at the unconscious level you have three kinds of information storage: Experiential Storage, Word Storage, and Conceptual Storage. You may think that the second and third types of storage are largely concerned with thought, whereas the first is not. But this is not entirely true. Above certain primitive—though vitally important—levels of brain function (I am referring to such things as automatic monitoring of the heart rate, balance correction, and so on), the brain must translate all experience into thought. Every experience that we have had since about the age of two has caused us to think thoughts. In this sense, thoughts constitute an important part of our Input.

I am sure you will have realized that what I have been driving at all along is that the parts of your brain which function at the unconscious level constitute the most fantastic, phenomenal—think of any adjective you want to and it still will hardly be adequate—type of computer known, the human biocomputer.

And what is the main Output of this marvelous biocomputer? It is your habits: 99 percent of what you do every day is done as a matter of habit. For some reason, people generally limit the meaning of the word *habit,* quite often to the extent of recognizing only a physical act as a "matter of habit." Ironically, I would think that the expression "He has the *bad* habit of . . ." is used ten times more frequently than the expression "He has the *good* habit of . . ." How quick we are to see the faults of others. Anyway, I want you to realize that if I say that 99 percent of everything you do is done as a matter of habit, I am being cautious. The fact of the matter is that the percentage is probably close to 99.9 percent.

A *Positive Attitude* is a matter of habit. *Confidence* is a matter of habit. *Enthusiasm, Self-discipline, Decisiveness, Diligence*—to name only a few of the matters we will be discussing all are habits—Output controlled by your biocomputer.

How do we form our habits? In our biocomputers there are programs. Obviously, there are *different* sets of programs in every biocomputer. There aren't the same programs in my biocomputer as is in yours, and there aren't the same in yours as in President Jimmy Carter's. But that is what makes each of us unique.

What is a program? It is a set of stored information and instructions. The programming process, the storing of information and instructions, commenced the instant you were born and it will continue until you die.

Yet one tragedy of life is that the vast majority of people have received their programming in a haphazard, hit-or-miss way, with very little control over the mechanics involved. The exciting thing about Cybernetics is that it has shown that, while we are all programmed, the status quo does not have to be maintained. Our programs are not unalterable. There are simple—although by no means obvious—techniques not only to replace bad habits with good ones, but even to acquire habits of such extraordinary power and effectiveness that most of us never dreamed they were possible.

If I were to try to explain these techniques to you right now, you probably would not believe me. They would seem at once too simple and too illogical. Yet after I have given you a few more facts about the cybernetic nature of your amazing biocomputer, I think you will see exactly how and why these techniques *have* to work.

A moment ago, in the context of habits or Output from the biocomputer, I mentioned Positive Attitude, Confidence, etc., which is Word Storage, and to which is integrated the relevant Conceptual Storage.

The personality of an individual is the sum total of all that person's habits or characteristics. The word *habit* is derived from the Latin word *habitus,* meaning *dress.* Our habits, our characteristics are the mantle of our personality. In the conglomeration of habits in which our individuality is dressed, there is a mixture of good, productive habits and poor, unproductive habits.

For example, look at the following (very partial) list of biocomputer Outputs, all of which, to a lesser or greater degree, you already have:

Confidence	Good Judgment	Punctuality
Energy	Outgoing	Authority and
Do It Now	Personality	Conviction
Diligence	Aggressiveness	Persistence
Decisiveness	Concentration	Creativity and
Resilience	Physical	Productivity
Discipline	Relaxedness	Empathy
Self-Reliance	Positive	Patience
Enthusiasm	Attitude	

Let us discuss the opposite of "Punctuality" which is the deplorable habit of "Tardiness" and see if we do not have the same Conceptual Storage in our respective biocomputers.

Tardy people are people who are careless and thoughtless about time. They are always late for appointments. They say they will do something by a certain time and then do not do it. Is this not the Conceptual Storage in your biocomputer relative to "Tardiness"?

The opposite of having a "do it now" attitude is "procrastination." The Conceptual Storage in my biocomputer relative to "procrastination" is someone who puts off doing something he knows he should have done, without having a valid reason. Doesn't his behavior correspond to the Conceptual Storage in your biocomputer relative to procrastination?

The reason I want to make sure that you understand Conceptual Storage is that the biocomputer does not process and act upon Input information word by word, but concept by concept. As we saw earlier when the electrode prevented CH from saying "foot," his biocomputer nevertheless processed the information conceptually.

People who want to be more successful in society must monitor the Output from their biocomputer and be sure that the twenty-one habits listed above represent the dominant Output from their biocomputers. That is not saying that *all* the unproductive Output must disappear (that would be poppycock), but people must be aware that if, for instance, their *dominant* Output were laziness and not diligence, then they would have *an incorrect program in their biocomputers.*

How do we go about changing such an incorrect program for the better? Most people, I imagine, would answer that question by saying: "through willpower." But reasonable as that might sound, it is quite wrong. For this purpose, willpower alone is practically useless. The key techniques for re-programming a biocomputer—techniques I call "Psychofeedback" and "RASCON"—are radically different from the use of willpower in that they require almost no effort at all. They are essentially automatic, which, as it happens, is one of the reasons why they are so effective.

What are these miraculous techniques and how can we make them work for us? That is the important subject we shall begin to take up in the next chapter.

4 Psychofeedback

Norbert Wiener, the father of Cybernetics, was also responsible for originating one of the central concepts of the new science. That concept is known as *Feedback,* and here is how Wiener defined it in his 1950 book, *The Human Use of Human Beings:*

> *FEEDBACK is a method of controlling a system [man or machine] by reinserting into it the results of its past performance.*

Such a simple definition of an apparently simple idea! And yet Pierre de Latil, one of Wiener's friends, tells us that Wiener eventually proclaimed the concept of Feedback as nothing less than "the secret of life. . . ."

What did the cool and rational Wiener find in this concept that so excited him and led him to make such an extravagant claim? In this chapter we shall try to answer that question; but first I think it would be a good idea if we agree on a point of terminology.

Ever since the middle sixties, biofeedback, as it has come to be called—has been the subject of the most intensive laboratory research all over the world. This research has involved the use of electromechanical devices which pick up and amplify body signals, electrical in their content, and convert them to a recognizable signal. (You can look at a piece of electric wire without knowing if it is alive or dead. The electricity must be converted to something you can see or hear, perhaps to the hand on a dial or the illumination of a lamp or a sound.) The person who is connected to the device can alter that signal and, in so doing, alter the body functions that produced it.

The results obtained by using these electromechanical devices have done nothing less than cause a revolution in medicine and psychology. They have shown us how to control certain body functions we supposed were beyond our control. We were taught that we, like other animals, had two nervous systems: the voluntary nervous system and the involuntary or autonomic nervous system. We were taught that it was with the voluntary nervous system that we had conscious control over our muscular system and its nerves. The rest of our anatomy—our heart, blood pressure, respiration, glandular activity, and so on—was beyond conscious control, the province of the autonomic nervous system. This system was a law unto itself—controlled by the brain, to be sure, but by that part of the brain which functions at the unconscious level.

Thus, when reports started coming in of individuals learning consciously to control different body functions, they sounded too incredible to be true. Finally the press and general public sat up and took notice with psychologist Joe Kamiya's article in *Psychology Today* (January 1968). Kamiya had devised a method whereby individuals would alter and, more important, *control* their own brain waves. From that moment, there was a surge of research, targeted exclusively at the theraputic applications of biofeedback. Some of the results were sensational.

By 1973 biofeedback was being hailed as a startling system for alleviating insomnia, anxiety, high blood pressure, muscular tics, headaches, asthma, and many other physical complaints; as a way of gaining mastery over our normal ongoing bodily processes; and as a revolutionary method of getting quickly in touch with the inner self—something yogis and Zen masters have been doing for centuries.

And, all these claims were true.

Because of the excitement which continues to be generated over biofeedback, which exclusively relies on electromechanical devices for its implementation, with the entire emphasis being placed on the medical and therapeutic benefits, a certain kind of Conceptual Storage is being established relative to it in the minds of many people. If we are not careful, we will lose sight of the magnitude of the importance of this mechanism.

We must realize that we use this mechanism every day of our lives without the aid of electromechanical devices. There is another aspect of it which demands that we distinguish it from what is now considered the orthodox biofeedback concept described above. Consequently, I have felt the need to use another expression to describe this mechanism as it relates to purposeful actions. I call it the only thing it can be called, which is PSYCHOFEEDBACK, and which I define thus:

> **Psychofeedback** *is a method of controlling the human system (and only the human system) by both reinserting into it the results of its past performance (as with orthodox feedback concepts) and by inserting into it the results of its present performance or experience.*

I can, with certainty, assure you that the way you have used your Psychofeedback mechanism to this date has determined how successful you have been in your career, and how much money you have earned. The way you continue to use it will determine how much money you will earn this year, next year, and the rest of your life.

The way you use this mechanism determines how well, or poorly, you play golf, tennis, bowling, or any other recreational activity you may be involved in.

The way you use this mechanism determines how fat or thin you are, assuming there is no physiological malfunction.

It is this mechanism, Psychofeedback, which ensured that we did not meet with physical and emotional catastrophe soon after we left the playpen. You may think that I am exaggerating the importance of the Psychofeedback mechanism. I only wish there were stronger words I could use because, in fact, it is this mechanism which ensures the survival of the human species, or any other species, for that matter.

Think of a child learning to feed itself. It knows that its food is on the plate and that it must transfer the food to its mouth. But the way it handles the spoon is very clumsy. At first, the child can only bring the food to the *general area* of its mouth. But every time it goes through the action correctly, that information is stored in its biocomputer. By continually reinserting the results of its past performance into its biocomputer, the child very quickly and efficiently has learned to feed itself.

Now the child is two or three years old, a toddler. It sees a bright, shining object and is attracted to it. The child grasps the object—a sharp knife—and cuts himself. Does it carelessly grasp the knife again? No. It uses its Psychofeedback mechanism. It has the ability to reinsert into its biocomputer the results of its past performance. The results of grasping the knife were blood and pain, and it stores this information.

One more example, this time with a slight difference. Now the child is older, say five or six, and is caught stealing cookies. Stealing is a no-no and the child is spanked. Does it steal the cookies again? Perhaps it does. Now there are two elements involved in the Psychofeedback mechanism: On the one hand is the memory of the delicious cookies that tasted so good; on the other hand, a sore bottom. But now the child's intellect has developed enough to use another faculty: that of *Judgment*. We shall have more to say about this all-important faculty later, but for the moment let us return to Psychofeedback.

The famous Russian physician Pavlov demonstrated the principle of conditioned reflexes by feeding dogs and ringing a bell at the same time. After a while it was necessary only to ring the bell in order to make the dogs salivate, even though no food was present. Ever since, psychologists have been fascinated by the implications of giving pleasure and inflicting pain, of reward and punishment.

I wonder if there is anyone who hasn't heard or read about the classic experiment where rats are put into a maze with food at the end. First it takes them a long time to find their way through the maze before reaching their reward. Each time they run the maze, they use their Psychofeedback mechanism—they reinsert into their bio-computer the results of their past performance—until finally the rats are able to run through the maze at great speed, barely making a mistake. In this case, the reward—the food at the end of the maze—provided the *motivation* for the rats to make efficient use of Psycho-feedback in their biocomputers. In another experiment, they could be motivated *not* to enter the maze if the result was certain punishment.

So far, I have no doubt that you have had no difficulty in following and accepting the things I have been saying about the type of Input known as Psycho-feedback. But how does this magnificent mind mechanism help us to achieve our objectives? If I were simply to state the next point I want to make, you might very well not believe me. So, rather than run that risk, I am going to give you the proof first and make the statement afterward.

In order to give you the necessary proof, I am going to have to ask for your cooperation. I should like you to conduct a simple experiment. I think you will find it surprising, and I assure you that the point it makes is very important—perhaps one of the most important to be made in this book.

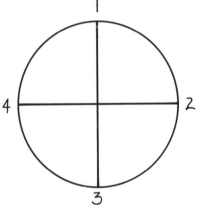

Fig. 2   Diagram for weight-and-string experiment

Figure 2 shows a diagram which you are asked to copy on a plain sheet of paper.

Find a very thin piece of string about 12 to 14 inches long and attach a metal object to the end of it. The best choice is a ¼-inch plumber's washer, or it can be a key, anything which is heavy enough to pull the string **straight.**

Now sit at a table, hold the string between your thumb and forefinger as illustrated in Figure 3, leaving about 10 or 11 inches of string between your thumb and the weight. Rest your elbow comfortably on the table, holding the weight over the point where the two lines

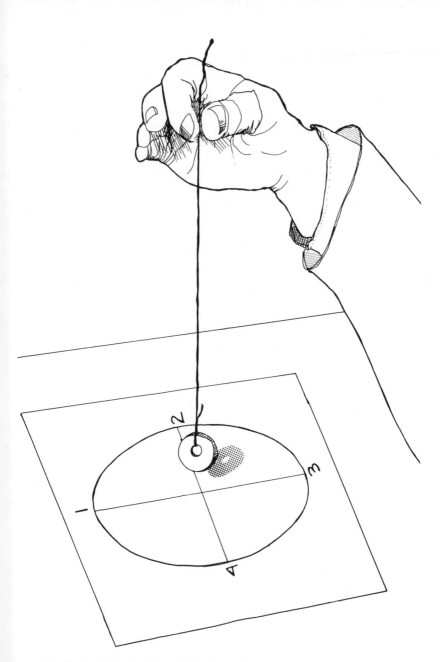

Fig. 3 Relative positions of hand, weight, and diagram

cross and about ½ inch above that point. *Do not move your hand*. Look at the weight and, without taking your eyes off the weight, *imagine* that the weight is moving—backward, forward, backward, forward, between the points numbered 1 and 3. Say the words to yourself. "Backward, forward, backward, forward, 1-3, 1-3, 1-3." Persistently and continuously repeat the words to yourself and imagine the direction of the movement of the weight.

Even though you do not move your hand, the weight will begin to swing between 1 and 3.

After you have the weight going with a good and pronounced movement backward and forward, *do not move your hand,* but change your thoughts only and *imagine* that the weight is going left, right, left, right, 4-2, 4-2, 4-2. Follow the same procedure for a circular clockwise movement—i.e., 1-2-3-4, 1-2-3-4—or counterclockwise—i.e., 4-3-2-1, 4-3-2-1. When you want the weight to stop moving, stop using your imagination and think about something entirely different.

If you have done this correctly, the weight will have moved as prescribed. This *must happen;* the amount of movement you obtained will have depended only upon your ability to concentrate.

I shall explain the point of this experiment shortly. But in order to do so I must first give you a little background information about how your nervous system works and then ask you to perform a second experiment.

The brain consists of tens of billions* of neuron cells, of different sizes and shapes. For everything that you do, every movement that you make, every thought that you think, everything that you sense—see, smell, taste, hear, and touch—there is, stored in your brain, an equivalent neuron chain. Chains or groups of neurons are called *ganglia.*

---

*Many writers say that the brain consists of about 10 billion neurons, and yet, even as an estimate, this cannot

Every neuron cell has a resting electrical potential, a voltage; it rests at something between 75 and 90 milivolts, negative: a milivolt is .001 of a volt. Furthermore, every neuron has the ability to generate, within itself, electricity and to alter its voltage. The generation of this electricity results from the differential permeability of an interface to the elements potassium and sodium.

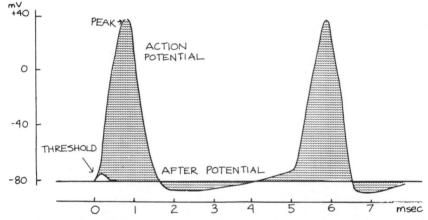

Fig. 4 Information is transmitted along neuron chains in the form of waves of altered electrical potential (called *action potentials*) that can travel at speeds of up to 300 feet per second

When a neuron is called upon to form a link in the neuron chain, it generates electricity within itself and alters its voltage. When it reaches a certain threshold it must "fire" or pulse, changing its polarity from negative to positive, then back to negative.

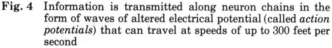

possibly be so. As Dr. Gordon Shepherd, professor of physiology at Yale, writes in his book *The Synaptic Organization of the Brain:* "It is commonplace to cite an estimate of 10 billion neurons. Those who cite this figure invariably fail to recall or realize that the number of granule cells in the cerebellum is probably several times this number."

All during the time that a neuron is a link in an active neuron chain, it continues to generate electricity, alternating between negative and positive at frequencies varying from .5 cycles, or times, per second up to 30 cycles per second. This range of frequency of firing of neuron cells is divided into the four brain rhythms—delta, theta, alpha, beta.

With this in mind let us return to our experiment with the string and weight.

Again, hold the string between your thumb and forefinger, but this time do not rest your elbow on the table and ignore the diagram completely. Position your hand in the middle of and against your chest, then move your hand and arm about 12 inches away from your chest. Return your hand to your chest. Again, move your hand and arm about 12 inches away from your chest and return it. Repeat this three or four times.

You have just *physically* moved the string and weight backward and forward. As you moved your arm, a certain number of neurons in your brain which are concerned *only* with that movement were activated and firing. If they had not fired, you would have been unable to move your hand and arm.

So now again hold the string between your thumb and forefinger, positioning your hand about 12 inches away from your chest. Do not rest your elbow on a table. Ignore the diagram.

Again, look at the weight and only *imagine* that the weight is going backward, forward, backward, forward. Repeat that over and over to yourself until you again obtain a good movement. When you imagined a movement of the weight, the *same* neurons fired again as those which were firing while you were actually and physically making the movement.

When they fired the second time, when the electrical activity commenced in your brain as a result of your imagining a movement, the electrical signal was transmitted down through your nervous system causing minute muscle movement in your hand. Too small to see, even too small to feel—but big enough to be picked up by the string which is sensitive to the smallest variations in the position of your hand.

In both experiments, as I am sure you will have noticed, the key factor was your imagination.

Interesting, you say, but does this have any practical application? Let me tell you about just one.

The following is a report which was published in *Industrial Research* magazine in December 1972.

> ## BIOELECTRICAL HAND DEVELOPED BY SOVIETS
>
> *Moscow—A type of prosthesis, quite new in principle—the bioelectrical hand—has been constructed in the Soviet Union by scientists of the U.S.S.R. Institute of Prosthetics and Prostheses Construction. Already licenses for manufacturing the new prosthesis have been purchased by Britain, France, Canada, and other countries.*
>
> *Currents produced in the nerve cells of the human body are used to operate the prosthesis. The person using it does not need to make any movement, he merely* imagines *[emphasis mine] the movement and the resultant biocurrent impulses make the mechanical hand work."*

When I read this report I must say that I was fascinated because Wiener had predicted just such a prosthetic device more than twenty years earlier.

Here, briefly, is how the artificial hand works. Imagine that you have a glass in your hand. Grip the imaginary glass tightly. Now stop gripping it. Again grip it tightly. You will have felt the muscles in your forearm tightening as you tightened your grip on the glass. An amputee can do the same thing. Although he has lost his hand and wrist, he has a "phantom hand." If electrodes are placed on the skin of the amputee's stump, one on the flexor muscle and one on the extensor, these pick up the minute electrical signals from the muscles. A case is fitted over the stump and is connected to an artificial hand. Inside the hand is a small electric motor driven by batteries.

The motor in the hand unit is two directional. When the motor drives forward, the hand opens; when it drives in reverse, the hand closes. What the bioelectrical current from the stump does, after it has been amplified, is to control the direction of drive of the motor. When the amputee *imagines* opening his hand, the motor, via the bioelectrical current, is switched to drive forward and the hand opens. When he *imagines* closing his hand the bioelectrical current switches the motor to reverse drive and the hand closes. If the muscles of the forearm of the amputee are wasted due to inactivity, and he cannot generate enough electrical potential on the skin surface to control the drive motor, he can be trained to use his imagination so that he can use other muscles in his anatomy, even muscles in the trunk!

However, interesting and eminently practical as the bioelectrical hand may be, it is nothing more than a dramatic but isolated illustration of the role imagination plays in the mechanism of Psychofeedback. Overwhelmingly more important are the uses we constantly make of imagination and Psychofeedback in the day-to-day conduct of our lives. Here are some examples.

Tonight, when you go to bed, you will probably decide to wake up at an hour which will enable you to achieve your goal of arriving at your place of work at a certain time. Suppose you live in the North and that tonight, on the radio or TV, you receive information that a heavy snowstorm is expected during the night—the first snow of the winter. If you have lived in the North long enough, you will have experienced other heavy snowstorms, and you will refer the information to Experiential Storage. You can imagine what it will be like tomorrow, and using Psychofeedback, you reinsert into your biocomputer the results of your past experience. Knowing that traveling to work will take much longer, you adjust your behavior accordingly and alter the time you will wake up.

But suppose you were from the South and had never experienced a snowfall, light or heavy. In other words, you have no Experiential Storage; you cannot *re*insert any information. What do you do? You get as much information as you can from other sources. You are able to *imagine* what the conditions will be like. You are *still able* to use your Psychofeedback mechanism by inserting *that* information, adjusting your behavior, and changing the time you wake up. You will still achieve the goal of arriving at your work at the time you wanted to be there. You are not dependent on your past performance.

If you travel to work on crowded buses or trains, you don't have to have had your purse snatched or your pocket picked in order to adjust your behavior so that your goal of getting to work unmolested will be achieved. In your biocomputer is Conceptual Storage related to "Traveling to work in the rush hour on a crowded train." By using your *imagination,* you can insert into your biocomputer what the results will be of your present performance if you are careless with your wallet or handbag. You use Psychofeedback and accomplish your goal.

During the course of the day, you will use your Psychofeedback mechanism constantly, reinserting via your Experiential Storage the results of your past performance and, via your imagination, inserting the results of your present performance. The entire process will be goal oriented. Some of the goals you may regard as trivial; others, as very important indeed. But without using your imagination you could not achieve many of them, and without using Psychofeedback, you could not achieve any of them.

A few pages back I said that I wanted to make a

vitally important point about the nature of Psychofeedback. But since I was afraid you might not believe me, I said I would give you the proof of what I intended to say before actually saying it. By now I hope that you have all the proof you need and that when I state my point, you will find it neither surprising nor unbelievable but, instead, obvious.

The point is this: *For practical purposes, the biocomputer cannot tell the difference between a real and an imagined experience.*

We do not have to have had an experience to use Psychofeedback efficiently. Of all creatures on the planet, man is the only one not dependent on past performance to control his future.

It is so marvelously elegant, so simple, so easy, that until it has been proven to them, most people have difficulty in accepting the logic of this truth. But the fact* remains that this is the sovereign mechanism that places the power for change in the hands of the individual, and allows him to control his destiny.

When an individual has *decided upon his goal* and when he can imagine *in a certain way* and *under certain*

---

*This fact was used to great effect during World War II by the distinguished British psychiatrist William Sargant, M.D., for the treatment of war neuroses.

The technique used with both military and civilian people who had collapsed, the former from battle, the latter from V-bomb explosions, was to make them relive, under drugs, the experience and abreact the same emotions. Dr. Sargant discovered that much better results could be obtained by stirring up emotions from *imaginary* happenings than by making them relive the actual happenings. For example, if a soldier had broken down as the result of a tank battle, it would be suggested to him under drugs that he was now trapped in a burning tank and must fight his way out. Though this situation had really never occurred it achieved the goal of returning the patient to mental health.

conditions that he has already reached his goal, that the goal has been accomplished, he is inserting (not reinserting) the results of his *present* performance* into his biocomputer. The biocomputer acts accordingly and makes every effort to take him to his goal.

By selling X volume of business, I will earn Y amount of money and I will be able to do Z. Whatever Z is, another car, another house, a trip around the world, whatever it is that I will spend the money for—that is the result of my *present* performance.

By eating X food, I will lose Y pounds and I will look like Z. In this case, Z is looking slim and trim, but still the result of my *present* performance. Regardless of whether the goal be a financial or career goal, a personal goal, physical goal, a family goal or, for that matter, a spiritual goal, the principle is the same. The success you will have in achieving the goals I shall ask you to set for yourself later in this book, will depend *only* on the efficiency with which you use your Psychofeedback mechanism.

In this chapter we have examined some of the secrets of our astonishing Psychofeedback mechanisms. In the next chapter we shall learn some equally extraordinary things about the ways we store information.

---

*The word "performance" is interchangeable with the word "experience."

5 Input Equals Output

It has always seemed to me that one of Norbert Wiener's major concerns was finding out if Cybernetics—the comparative study—could help the lame of our society. Having pointed out that malfunctions in computer systems are not entirely dissimilar to malfunctions of the brain, Wiener hypothesized:

> *In a system containing a large number of neurons, circular processes can hardly be stable for long periods of time. Either, as in the case of storage* belonging to the specious* present, it runs its course, dissipates itself, and dies out,** *or it com-*

---

*Fictitious or false. There is no "present"; there is only a past or a future. For there to be a "present," time would have to stand still!
**My emphasis. P.T.

prehends more and more neurons in its system, until it occupies an inordinate part of the neuron pool. This is what we should expect to be the case in the malignant worry which accompanies anxiety neurosis. In such a case, it is probable that the patient simply does not have the room, the suffi- cient number of neurons, to carry out his normal processes of thought.* *Under such conditions, there may be less going on in the brain to load up the neurons not yet affected, so that they are all the more readily involved in the expanding process.*

Furthermore, the permanent storage becomes more and more deeply involved, and the pathologi- cal process which occurred at first at the level of the circulating storage may repeat itself in a more intractable form at the level of the permanent stor- age. Thus what started as a relatively trivial and accidental reversal of stability [of thought] may build itself up into a process totally destructive to the ordinary mental life.

In the foregoing, Wiener made *two* very important state- ments, the significance of which must not elude you because together, they are the keys to all human en- deavor.

To understand and grasp the significance of the first of these, I must ask you to remember one of the two ways that a mechanical computer can do what it does: it is by having *stored information.* We have already seen that we have three kinds of storage in the biocomput- er: Word Storage, Experiential Storage, and Conceptual Storage. Weiner points out that there are further classifi- cations:

Circulating Storage, which, as Wiener puts it, "deals with the specious present, dissipates itself and dies out."

---

*My emphasis. P.T.

Permanent Storage, which dies only with the death of the individual.

We are what we are, we have reached the station in life that we we have reached, we are as happy or unhappy as we are because of the Permanent Storage that is in our biocomputer. Only by making sure that the correct Permanent Storage is in your biocomputer and combining it with efficient use of Psychofeedback will you stand a chance of achieving your potential.

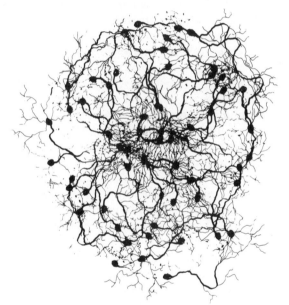

Fig. 5 A neuron chain

For everything that we do, every thought that we think, every movement we make, everything we sense—see, smell, hear, taste, and touch—there is a neuron chain. It is a little difficult to conceptualize the incredible weaving and interweaving of the neurons, with their axons and dendrites, which make up a neuron chain. This is not only because of their huge numbers and complex patterns, but also because of the infinitesimally small distances involved. Nevertheless, I do want you to try to picture to yourself, if only in a schematic way, what a neuron chain is like.

Neurons communicate with each other at points which are called synapses (see Figure 6).

The electron microscope has revealed that the synaptic organization in the brain is utterly amazing. As recently as the 1950's, the most adventurous authority would not dare to estimate a number higher than about 100 synapses per neuron. Now it is known that the numbers can be in the tens of thousands on one neuron—now that is something really difficult to conceptualize, isn't it? In addition to this, the electron microscope has revealed that the different synaptic combinations—axon/dendrite/soma—is much more varied than was until recently believed to be the case.

It is through the action of the synapses, electrical and chemical, that decisions are made regarding the transmission (excitatory) or nontransmission (inhibitory) of information. It is not necessary in a book of this nature to go into the intricacies of the synapses, fascinating though they are. The importance of the synapses, as far as we are concerned, is that Circulating Storage becomes Permanent Storage as a result of modifications at the synapses which results in an increased capacity to conduct a transmitting, or excitatory, impulse. This increased capacity can result in two ways: by the habitual use of the synapses in a particular neuron chain or pathway, or as a result of the attention given by the RAS to details of a sequence of activities.

In a moment I am going to ask you to do things which will be examples of Circulating Storage, but before I do that, I want you to understand that I am not asking you to test your memory. As I have mentioned previously, we have a concept of "memory," i.e., remembering something, which is meaningless in the context of "stored information." All the time you are conscious, your bio-

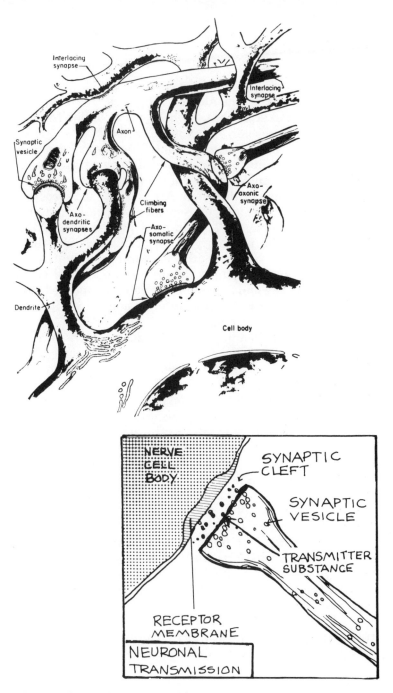

Fig. 6 Types of synapses and how they operate

computer is processing information, so when I ask you the question, "Are you able to *re*process the information?" I mean exactly that. To help you to understand, I will use the expression "Do you remember?" only once.

I want you to imagine something. Let us assume that you are driving along a very busy two-way street, with many cars going in the same direction as you, and many in the opposite direction. Are you able to reprocess the information, i.e., do you remember the cars going in the *opposite* direction *after* you have passed them? You most certainly do not. As you approach each car, that information, for which neuron chains are activated in your biocomputer, is vitally important, a matter of your life or death. The split second after you have passed the car coming toward you, the information is dissipated because it is *no longer* important.

As you are reading these words, for each word a neuron chain is being activated in your biocomputer. The neurons are firing across the synaptic gap. It is only a few seconds since you read the last paragraph. Are you able to reprocess the information now—at this moment—in such a way as to be able to repeat the paragraph word for word? Of course you cannot. But it is not important that you can. It was only important that you understood the *meaning* of the words. The biocomputer does not process information only word by word, but concept by concept.

In both examples, you processed the information with your eye sensors, but it is exactly the same with your ear sensors when you are involved in conversation. It is not important whether you can exactly reprocess the words you heard one minute ago. They are important only in the context of what you heard before and what you hear afterward.

I am sure you can reprocess the information relative to the events of the day as they happened *yesterday,* and probably in a fairly accurate sequence. Can you do the same for the events of this day of the month, one month ago? If you can, try six months ago. From the point of view of memory, you will say that you can not remember, which will be correct. However, and this is why I insist on the distinction between storage and memory, *everything to which you paid particular attention is still stored in your biocomputer.* The Circulating Storage, of course, has gone.

In Chapter III, we read about what had happened to the patients of Wilder Penfield as their brains were being electrically stimulated. Let us re-examine what happened with MMa.

"I was there and someone was calling me—a man leaning on a desk with a pencil in his hand." Penfield comments: All the details of those things *to which she had paid attention* in some previous period of time were still there. Perhaps the pencil in his hand had seemed important but other images that must have reached her retina during the original experience are now lost, probably *because they were ignored originally.*

A few years ago, the headlines contained a particularly dramatic illustration of this truth. On July 16, 1976, at Chowchilla, California, a particularly vicious crime was committed by three men. A school bus carrying 23 children between the ages of 7 and 12 was stopped on a lonely country road by three armed men wearing masks. The men kidnapped the children and bus driver, hurried them off the bus into a closed van, drove them some miles away to a quarry, transferred them to a furniture van and then buried the van, with the still-living children and bus driver in it. The authorities and police were baffled and desperate, not having a single clue to work with.

It was most fortunate that the kidnappers, presumably in their concern not to attract attention to themselves, only spent enough time to bury the van with a light covering of earth, because after hours of trying to attract attention to themselves with shouts for help, Ed

Ray, the bus driver, had the presence of mind to find a way to break out of the van. The kidnappers had neglected to secure a small ventilation cover in the roof of the van. Ray was able to force it open and one of the smaller children was able to clamber through and so bring rescuers before the kidnappers could make their ransom demand.

The driver and children could only tell the police the bare facts of the event. They could give no adequate description of the men or the van in which they were taken to the quarry. Ed Ray had read the license plate number of the van, but, try as he could, he could not remember the number.

After hours of questioning the police concluded that the victims would be of no assistance to them, and they had to rely exclusively on the clues at the quarry. But weeks of fruitless investigation almost brought them to the point of admitting defeat. Then Sheriff Ed Bates, who was in charge of the case, remembered that the Los Angeles Police Department had used hypnosis to solve a number of crimes when victims of, or witnesses to, crimes had been unable to remember details. Ed Ray was hypnotized, and in a state of hypnosis he repeated the license plate number of the van *correct to one digit*. Within the hour the police were at the home of the owner of the van, who, of course, was one of the kidnappers.

How long do you think Ed Ray looked at the plate number? Probably only for a moment. But when he looked at it, Ed Ray's mind, the operator of his biocomputer, said with intensity, "I must remember." A neuron chain was formed and the information went into Permanent Storage as a result of the electro-chemical activity across the synaptic gaps of the neurons in the chain.

Another, more personal example: Some years ago I was asked to speak to an annual meeting of the Southern California P.G.A. In case you are not a golfer, I should explain that there are two kinds of golf professionals:

playing professionals who are on the tour, and teaching professionals who spend most of their time teaching the amateurs. It was to the teaching professionals that I gave a lecture on the importance of Cybernetics as it relates to golf, with the result that many of the 130 who attended the meeting went on to complete my course of instruction. A student in one of these classes was Tom Barber, who is one of the teachers at Griffith Park golf course, a fine golfer, twice the four ball champion of Southern California, and from 1975 to 1978, chairman of the S.C.P.G.A. player division.

At the end of the fourth lesson of the class in which Tom was a student, he came to me and asked if it would be possible for him to see me in my office for a private talk. He was very diffident as he said, "I've had a problem for a number of years which I've never talked to anyone about. I think you may be able to help me to solve it. Actually, I feel kind of ridiculous even talking about it."

After I had given him what reassurances I could, he said, "Look, it's irrational and illogical, I know, but I have a fear of the dark!" He went on to explain that this had started when he was about fifteen, that the night, as such, had no effect on him, it was only on going to bed that, within a few minutes of turning off the light, he would start to experience irrational fears. On such occasions he would feel compelled to switch on the light and would only be able to go to sleep if the light remained lit. As a result of beginning to understand the mechanics of his own mind and his biocomputer, it had seemed obvious to him that, somewhere, in his Permanent Storage, there had to be some information which was the cause of his problem. I agreed that it couldn't be otherwise.

Although Tom was able to resolve his problem before the end of the course, we were both curious to know what the storage was that was causing his problem. It so happens that Tom is one of those fortunate people who can easily be taken into a very deep state of hypnosis, so, subsequently, after the eighth lesson, I hypnotized him to a degree that permitted us to use the same time regression technique that was used with Ed Ray. The result was as follows: One night when Tom was five years old, his mother had left him and his three-year-old sister alone in the house when she went to the market. Before his mother had returned, someone knocked at the front door. When the children did not answer, the caller had gone to the back door and this time knocked louder and more persistently. It was probably nothing more ominous than a neighbor, who, seeing the lights, could not understand why there was no response. But by this time the two children, really frightened, had switched off the lights and hidden under the table, where their mother found them when she returned from the market.

When Tom was brought out of hypnosis he said, "Well, I'll be damned! I had completely forgotten about that!"

I repeat, I am what I am, and you are what you are, because of the Permanent Storage that is in our biocomputers.

Before explaining the second part of Wiener's hypothesis, I must remind you of the second way that a mechanical computer can do what it does: by having an Input and an Output.

We have already established that our Input has been, is, and always will be, our thought. What is it that every experience we have had since about the age of two has caused us to do? These experiences have caused us to think thoughts. But how is it, according to Wiener's hypothesis, that a person becomes afflicted with the burden of anxiety neurosis? It is a result, in Wiener's words, of "a relatively trivial and accidental reversal of stability" of *thought,* causing an interruption in the *"normal processes of thought."*

If it weren't so distressing for some people, I would find it ironic that the computer industry has coined an expression which is particularly apt and fitting: "Garbage in, Garbage out." It is obviously the same with the human brain. Bad thoughts produce bad Output; good thoughts, good Output.

Of course, as a concept, positive thinking has been with us for a long time. Two thousand years ago it was said, "As a man thinketh, so is he."

Most self-improvement books, such as *Think and Grow Rich* by Napoleon Hill, or *The Power of Positive Thinking* by Norman Vincent Peale, or *The Magic of Thinking Big* by David Schwartz, stress the importance of thinking the correct thoughts. In fact, "You've got to think positive" has become a cliché of our society.

Yet, with all due respect to the fine authors mentioned above, their work does not explain the mechanism involved in the thinking process. Without exception, they urge their readers not to question how thinking positively will help them; the degree of trust which they call for is beyond most people's capacity.

Writing in a completely different context and with a different purpose in mind, Wiener gave us the explanation quite clearly. It is that a negative thought has the ability, neurologically, to attract to it similar thoughts. The corollary of this is that a positive thought must have the same ability.

It follows logically that there must be a kind of specially structured Input or "thought formula" that can *reverse* the process described by Wiener—a "thought formula" that instead of afflicting a person with the burden of anxiety neurosis will elevate him to confident productivity, peace of mind, and happiness.

This *sounds* very much like what Hill, Peale, Schwartz, and other popular self-help writers have been saying. But, unlike the others, Wiener did not arrive at his conclusion intuitively. Rather, it was based on rigorous logic, vast scientific knowledge, and a profound understanding of how "thinking machines" operate. This

difference becomes particularly important when it comes
to defining precisely what the "positive thought formula"
must be. For plainly, in order to work, any such formula
has to be cybernetically correct if it is to become Permanent Storage in the biocomputer. If your reaction to the
foregoing is still one of skepticism on the grounds that
Wiener, however accomplished he may have been in his
own field of mathematics, was not really a brain specialist, you may be interested to learn that modern brain
research has, in fact, confirmed all his basic insights and
predictions.

For example, Professor Roger Sperry of the California Institute of Technology has conclusively proven that
individual neurons develop the ability to recognize one
another by acquiring "individual identification tags, molecular in nature." In action, an "identification tag" can
be passed across a synaptic gap from one neuron to
another. "As a result of this process," writes Professor
George Ungar of the Baylor College of Medicine, "the two
neurons recognize each other and their junction creates a
new pathway."

This, of course, amounts to a physiological explanation of how Wiener's hypothesis about anxiety neurosis would work. Neurons carrying repetitive thought
patterns have the power—through transfer of "identification tags"—to involve more and more neurons in their
habitual activity. If the thought patterns are negative,
they may thus be strengthened to the point of becoming a
dangerous neurosis. By the same token, if an individual's
habitual thought patterns are positive, his brain contains
an automatic neuronal mechanism whereby these positive thoughts can be augmented until they become over-
whelmingly powerful.

But perhaps all this would be clearer if I were to
give you some real-life examples. I should like to tell you
about three people of completely different backgrounds—
a woman and two men—who understood the enormous

advantages to be gained from this automatic augmentation of positive thought patterns and who therefore took special pains to control the Input into their biocomputers.

What happens to people when they understand the concepts set forth in Psychofeedback Seminars is so dramatic that I frequently get calls from individuals who are friends or relatives of my students. One such call came late in 1973. Karl Schillig explained that he had been under the care of a doctor for two years and that during those two years the doctor had prescribed Desbutal, a drug, which had not helped him. At the end of that time, his doctor had asked him to see a psychiatrist. Karl had seen the psychiatrist regularly for six months. At the end of that time, the psychiatrist, at a loss to understand why there was no improvement, gave Karl another prescription for the same Desbutal—this time a *double dose*.

Karl's difficulty was that, for no apparent reason and when he least expected it, he would be assailed with the blackest depression. Perhaps he would wake up so depressed that he would be unable to get out of bed, or perhaps he would be hit at work and would have to go home. He had a good job as a financial analyst with Litton, the California conglomerate, but his reputation within his company was deteriorating.

I told Karl that I was not engaged in the therapeutic field, that I had a new class starting each week, that he could listen to an introductory lecture, and that if then he wished to join the class, he could do so. Because of the strict California law related to the practice of medicine, I told him that at no time would I be in a position to discuss his problem privately.

Because of his original phone call, I was particularly interested in Karl's career, and about six months after he had completed the course I called him. I was delighted when he told me that his depression had completely disappeared. Furthermore, he said, he was quite sure that he would not have such experiences again. He was confidently looking for a better job.

After another six months, Karl called to tell me that he had achieved that goal and had landed a much better job with Occidental Petroleum. The next news I had of Karl was when I received this announcement card:

> *It is with great pleasure that Hollywood Proper-ties, Inc., announce the appointment of Karl (John) Schillig to its staff of professional Real Estate Counselors.*

As a result of the correct thought formula being inserted and *maintained* in Permanent Storage, and attracting to it similar storage, Karl became such a self-reliant and resilient person that he gave up the "security" of a salary to work on commission. In terms of success and psychic well-being, the results have been beyond anything he could previously have thought possible.

An aspect of Psychofeedback Seminars that I con-sider to be of the utmost importance is that husbands and wives should learn how to apply the principles of Cyber-netics to their lives together, and having done so, should continue to apply those same principles *together*. So important do I consider this, that I make a point of charging no additional tuition fee for a person to join his or her spouse in class. Thus it was that in February 1974, homemaker Jean Nelson joined her husband, Tom, a real estate salesman, in a course set up in his office. About four months after completing the course, I received this handwritten letter from Jean.

August 23, 1974

> *I do want to let you know how very much your Cybernetics course has meant to me.*
>
> *When I started your course it was with much apprehension. I'm sure I was the worst student in the whole class because of all my many fears. But,*

Paul, I honestly feel I received more benefit than anyone in the group. I'll tell you why.

For the past ten years I have been a very nervous and fearful person. I became afraid of some really dumb things—crowds, airports, new situations, ill health, and just about anything else you can think of. Needless to say my self-confidence became nonexistent. Just plain everyday living became almost impossible.

Well—let me tell you—even before I finished your course I was making great improvements. Since finishing the course, I've made even more.

I've enrolled in a real estate class, have enjoyed going out to dinner in crowded restaurants, and have even learned to like elevators again, and today I spent six hours in a crowded shopping center with my kids. Can you believe that?

These things may sound simple or silly to others—but to me it's absolutely thrilling. My self-confidence is growing every day. Occasionally I still get twinges of fear but they don't last long because every time a fearful thought comes to mind—I am aware of it and change my thoughts—ha—I love it!

Paul, I don't know how to thank you for what you've done for me. I feel like you've given my life back to me. Before Cybernetics I was just breathing and thinking negative thoughts.

My family and friends are amazed at the changes happening to me, but I know that this is just the beginning.

Sincerely,
Jean Nelson

P.S. I forgot to include the fact that during the past ten years, I've gone to doctors, therapists, self-help groups and nothing helped. Thanks again.

The day I received this letter, I telephoned Jean not only to tell her how pleased I was to hear from her, but also to ask her some questions about the contents of her letter. During the conversation I learned that the kind of crowd she referred to in her letter was the mid-morning or mid-afternoon "crowd" one sees in supermarkets. Formerly, she had to do her shopping at seven o'clock in the morning, rush round the market buying her groceries and then rush home to the "safety" of her home. This had been going on for ten years, and her husband knew nothing about her problems!

The "bad" Circulating Storage in Jean's biocomputer had gradually but ever-increasingly become Permanent Storage and made her life miserable. When Jean understood the Input/Output mechanism, put the correct thought formula as new Permanent Storage into her biocomputer and *maintained* it as Permanent Storage, her life was transformed.

Jean Nelson and Karl Schillig would readily admit that they both had the worst possible kind of Permanent Storage in their biocomputers. They had never controlled their thought processes. "Garbage" had gone into their biocomputers and "Garbage" came out. But since they are extreme examples, for my third illustration, let me go to the other extreme and tell you about a man who already had very good Permanent Storage in his biocomputer.

Dennis Fitzgerald was one of the most successful stockbrokers with the firm of Bateman, Eichler, Hill, Richards when he became one of my students in September 1975. In the previous seven years his gross annual commissions had never been less than $100,000. His best year had been 1972, a good year for the entire industry, when his gross commissions totaled $251,000.

The year after he completed the course—1976—the year which saw the stockmarket active in only the first three months of the year, saw the Dow Jones Industrial average slide from a high of 1020 to a low of 865, and saw many brokerage companies go bankrupt, Dennis grossed $265,000! In 1977, while the market was still in the doldrums, his gross was $350,000, and he was appointed to the board of directors of B.E.H.R. His long-term goal is to consistently trade an annual volume of securities which will gross $500,000.

I do not suggest for a moment that Dennis's spectacular success was due solely to what he learned in my course. What he learned from me was an improvement on what he was already doing. He learned to be even more aware of his own thoughts, which, in turn, made the already-excellent Permanent Storage in his biocomputer even better. By his own admission, he did have some poor storage in his biocomputer which had become permanent (it was related to a disastrous marriage a few years earlier), but he says that he put new Permanent Storage into his biocomputer related to this aspect of his life. By the time you read this, he will be happily married.

Your situation in life may not be similar to those of any one of the three people I have just described. But one thing is the same: When the correct "thought formula," the Input into your biocomputer, becomes part of your Permanent Storage and then attracts to it similar and related storage, some dramatic things will happen in your life.

As you doubtless already have guessed, this whole business of constructing and inserting correct Input is intimately connected to the extraordinary powers of your imagination and to the fact that your biocomputer cannot distinguish between "real" and imaginary Input. Let's look more closely now at the vital subject of imagination.

6 Using Your Imagination

Consider two brief quotations. Here is the first:

> We possess within us a force of incalculable power, which, when we handle it unconsciously is often prejudicial to us. If on the contrary we direct it in a conscious and wise manner, it gives us the mastery of ourselves and allows us not only to escape and to aid others to escape, from physical and mental ills, but also to live in relative happiness, whatever the conditions in which we may find ourselves.

Do these words sound contemporary to you? They should because if you watched National Geographic's television program *The Incredible Machine,* you would have heard Dr. Barbara Brown say something very similar.

> *We never thought that we could do this before. The*
> *implications are so vast, it's very difficult, I think,*
> *to describe what they all might be. I think they'll be*
> *in the area of learning to control various aspects of*
> *one's own mind, mental activity, and consciousness*
> *as well.*

Yet approximately one hundred years separates these two statements. The former was made by Emile Coué, a French pharmacist who, in the 1870's, became fascinated by the power of the mind as it related to health.

Around 1880 Coué gave up his profession, opened a free clinic at Nancy, and devoted himself to helping the sick. He effected many miraculous cures in his clinic and, by the turn of the century, had gained great fame in France. From there his reputation gradually spread throughout Europe; by the 1920's, he was an international celebrity. In 1922 Coué came to America on a lecture tour, but I am sad to say that it was a failure. To most Americans, the concepts which he propounded seemed too unscientific to be believable. They should have believed him, because what he said was absolutely true. In the light of our present knowledge of Cybernetics, the significance of Emile Coué's work comes across the span of years like a clarion call.

Coué's greatest insight was embodied in a law which he propounded and formalized in his book *Self-Mastery Through Conscious Autosuggestion:*

> *When the imagination and willpower are in con-*
> *flict, are antagonistic, it is always the imagination*
> *which wins,* without any exception.

This law, said Coué, is as immutable as the Law of Gravity. If that were so, one would have expected that it would be common knowledge. Yet of course it was not and is not. And I cannot emphasize too strongly that ignorance of Coué's Law is the reason that the vast majority of people are prevented from achieving their most clearly defined objectives. Let me give you some examples.

Think of a plank of wood 16 to 18 inches wide. This is approximately the distance from your elbow to the tip of your outstretched fingers—in other words, fairly wide. Imagine also that it is about 30 to 40 feet long. This plank is on the floor in front of you. Now walk the length of it without allowing your feet to come off the plank and touch the floor. Imagine that you are doing this. As you walk down the plank, you may glance down once or twice to check your general position, but you easily and casually saunter down its entire length and never touch the floor.

Now put the same plank six feet up in the air between two trestles and walk its length again. This time you do not take your eyes off the plank. There will probably be a very slight wobble in your leg movements, but you reach the end of the plank satisfactorily.

Now suspend this same wide plank three hundred feet up in the air between two buildings and walk its length again. This is probably what would happen. You would be teetering on the end of the plank, leaning backward and you would be imagining a very unpleasant red blotch on the sidewalk. Do you know what would happen if you started to move a foot? Your foot and leg, regardless of which one you stepped off with, would not go straight and parallel with the plank, it would go *sideways* and you would become that red blotch you were worrying about. Even if it were a very still day, without the whisper of a breeze anywhere, you, teetering on the end of the plank, would probably be thinking, "Oh God, supposing the wind blows!" In this case, if you started to move, you would likely go headfirst off the plank.

When the plank was on the floor, you zipped across it, surefooted. At six feet up, your legs wobbled a little because although there was no great conflict between

your imagination and willpower, there was some—you
could hurt yourself falling from six feet. But at three
hundred feet up, there was absolute conflict between your
two faculties. No amount of willpower would have taken
you across the plank. Because of Coué's Law, your imagination had to win. I might mention that there are some
people who couldn't walk across the plank if it were only
two feet off the floor. They do not realize it but they are
actually quite fortunate, as we will see in a moment.

Every New Year's Eve, millions of people decide
that they are going to stop smoking. This is their New
Year's resolution, they genuinely mean to do just that.
They get up on January first full of iron-jawed determina-
tion and willpower. They say to themselves over and over
again, "I'm not going to smoke, I'm not going to smoke, *I
am not going to smoke*"—and all the time they are imagining how good a cigarette would taste! Their resolve
might last for thirty minutes or thirty days, but finally
they succumb because they could not break Coué's Law.
Yet if they had understood the implications of Coué's
Law, they would have known there was an entirely different way to approach the problem that would have been
nearly effortless and would have succeeded.

Again, why is it so many people have difficulty in
losing weight? Perhaps we should start at the other end
and ask why people put on weight. They do so because
they indulge themselves. There is so much nonsense
spoken and written about "emotional problems" being
the cause of overeating: The primary cause of overeating
is that we enjoy food, and eating is one of the ways in
which we have a good time. But since people also enjoy
(or think they would enjoy) being slim, why is it that
people find it so difficult to lose the weight they ought to
lose? When they put themselves on diets which they
really do not enjoy, how long are they firm in their resolve? Two days? Three? Let's assume they are in their
fourth day and, perhaps, having a mid-morning coffee

break. They start imagining how good it would be to have a Twinkie or a Ring Ding! And when they fall by the wayside, they generally lament that they just don't have any willpower. Instead, they should say that they have an excellent imagination.

Do you play golf? If you do, how many times have you looked over your next shot and seen . . . the water. As you addressed the ball, you've probably said sternly to yourself, "I must not hit it in the water." So you hit the ball with a good stroke . . . and splash!

Every professional salesman knows it is axiomatic in his profession that if he wants to make sales he has got to make calls. The ruin of many a potential sales career— and, I might add, a continuous problem for the established career—is Coué's Law, which leads inevitably to what I describe as "call reluctance." Regardless of the product or service, every salesperson at some time experiences call reluctance. The person who says that he has never experienced it is full of—to put it politely—false bravado. Here's an example based on fact.

Mary has had her real estate license for about four months. She has been given a "farm," which is the term adopted by the industry instead of "territory," and she has been doing the things which she has been assured will result in her making sales and securing listings. She regularly does her mailings and spends three hours every day on her "farm" knocking on doors. But she does not enjoy it. On a particular Wednesday, she decides that she will not go out canvassing her "farm," but instead will work with the telephone that evening. Her realtor has a reverse directory (telephone directory where the names, addresses, and telephone numbers are not listed alphabetically but sequentially by house and street numbers), and at 6:00 P.M. sharp she is at her desk, the reverse street directory in front of her.

She looks down the first column, remembering the street, she gets to the end of the column, looks up to the top of the second column, reads slowly down the names and numbers to the end, then back up to the top of the third column. Halfway down the third column, while she is still staring intently at the page, she moistens her finger on her tongue and turns the page. It is 6:15, and she still hasn't made her first telephone call. She takes about ten minutes looking up and down the columns of the next page. Then, exasperated with herself, she turns back to the first page, picks a telephone number near the top of the first column, reaches for her telephone, dials the number and gets . . . a busy signal. She is secretly relieved.

Coué's Law has got her!

While she sat at her desk, perhaps only fleetingly, she imagined that maybe she would disturb the people she was calling; or, just as fleetingly, she imagined that the person she was calling would be rude and churlish. Her decision—"make telephone calls this evening"—was an act of willpower. Yet, at the moment of action, her imagination and her willpower were in conflict, and imagination had to prevail. From the moment that Mary decided she was going to do her prospecting on the telephone she should have persistently imagined that everyone she called would be very pleased to hear from her, regardless of the outcome of any particular call as she was making the calls.

There is nothing which will destroy your confidence in your ability faster or more completely than your imagination and willpower in conflict with each other. When sales directors and managers are urging their sales staff to make the calls, they would be well advised to counsel their staff of the immutability of Coué's Law and to teach the method of avoiding the trap. It does little good to talk in terms of "fear of rejection" or "fear of failure" or any of the other standard phrases which are used to describe this phenomenon.

Earlier this year, my wife and I were guests at a

delightful dinner party. Our hosts provided live music, and by the end of dinner, we were all singing along with the musician. I discovered that our hostess had a lovely singing voice. When I complimented her, she answered that I should have heard her when she was a girl. She said that she had once aspired to a singing career but had never been able to overcome her stage fright. I could not help wondering how many other aspiring young performers had had their ambitions thwarted because they neither understood the problem of imagination and will-power in conflict nor the remedy for it.

Because, happily, as with all laws, there *is* a corollary to Coué's Law. It is, very simply and logically that:

When the imagination and willpower are harmoniously pulling in the same direction, an irresistible force is the result.

If children were taught at the earliest age to understand Coué's Law and, more important, its corollary, there is no doubt that it would prevent millions from experiencing strife later in their lives, as the following will illustrate.

The changes which have taken place in our society in the past thirty years are enormous from many aspects. One of the aspects is that young people take on the stature of adulthood at a much earlier age. This is a result of them having information stored in their biocomputer, in effect vicarious Experiental Storage, which was never possible before television became a universal method of disseminating information. What was considered, not so long ago, as the period of adolescent youth is shrinking so fast as to be barely distinguishable. Young people are catapulted from childhood to adulthood but without the maturing process of personal Experiental Storage.

Inevitably this has caused teachers to face an entirely different environment to that of their forebears which is certainly not enhanced by the general lowering of standards of discipline. It has become axiomatic among teachers that the very first day of a new school year with a new group of students sets the seal on the relationship which will exist between teacher and students for the rest of the year. That if, on the first day, a bad relationship is established, then the students often refuse to work for the teacher and, perhaps worse, the immature young adults can drive a teacher into a state of harassment. One of my former students, Barbara Hamilton, was, and still is, a teacher at the Patrick Henry Junior High School. She teaches youngsters between the ages of 12 and 15 years and had been doing so for eight years prior to becoming my student. As do the vast majority of teachers, Barbara takes her profession very seriously.

Although she had never had a bad experience on a first day of the new school year, she had had the importance of the "first day" drummed into her by other teachers, and she had in fact seen student teachers bring disaster upon themselves by being careless on their first day with a new class.

For *eight years* previous to understanding Coué's Law, the unhappiest, most disturbing time of the year for Barbara were the 4 to 5 weeks between August and early September. She would spend the whole time worrying about what she would say, what she would do, even how she would dress on the "first day," because she *imagined* that awful things would happen if she were careless and said or did the wrong thing! Eight years of having her imagination and her willpower in conflict—of breaking Coué's Law. But since invoking the corollary of Coué's Law this has not happened.

Linda Tindaro is the director of advertising for a major land developer: "I have been asked on several occasions to speak before large groups. I would usually spend weeks worrying about what I would say and the effect I would have on my audience. By the time the meeting took place, I would be stiff, self-conscious, and would stumble over my words even though I knew my subject well"—thereby breaking Coué's Law.

During her third week in the course and after invoking the corollary, Linda continues: "I was asked once again to speak. I found myself full of confidence and anxious to tell this group my information. I was comfortable and able to field several difficult questions. I actually enjoyed speaking and found my audience responsive and enthusiastic. For me, this was a great accomplishment."

In the twilight of his life, Montaigne said something as chilling as it is true: "My life has been filled with terrible misfortune, most of which never happened!"

When we discussed Psychofeedback earlier, I said that it is by using your imagination in a *certain way* and under certain conditions that your mind mechanism operates most efficiently. There are two ways that a person is able to use his imagination: *objectively* and *subjectively*. When people use their imaginations objectively, it is as though they were looking at a screen and seeing a moving picture. They can "see" themselves doing something, but they do not really feel that they are participating in the action. For example, as I am writing this, I am in my studio, which is in the garden, separate from our house. I can imagine putting down my pen, pushing the chair back, standing up, walking through the French doors, stepping onto the concrete pathway, walking the ten or twelve feet of concrete past the lemon tree, turning left on the concrete, and walking to the back door. I imagined that, but I did it objectively. I was completely removed from the experience.

With a little more effort, I could have imagined the same thing subjectively. I could actually have felt and *experienced* the things I was imagining. If I were to go through the same motions I describe above, I would have to stop writing and close my eyes because I find it almost impossible to use my imagination subjectively with my eyes open. But having done so, as I imagined walking across the studio, I would have *felt* the carpet. When I got to the concrete, I would have *felt* the hardness through my shoes. I would have *smelled* the lemon tree as I passed it. In this way my imaginary experience would have come as close to reality as possible.

There is only one major group of people who consistently employ subjective imagination. That group is comprised of children under the age of seven. When a little boy is in his soapbox racer, what he is riding is not a soapbox to him, but a Ferrari or Maserati. And it isn't the downgrade of 26th Street that he is on, it is the track of the Indy 500 or Le Mans. When a little girl plays with her doll, it is not a doll that she dresses and takes for walks, it is her baby.

Unfortunately, few of us continue to make use of this capacity for intense subjective imagination after we have left childhood behind us. Neither our educational system nor our society as a whole has recognized the value of subjective imagining. In fact, schools have systematically tended to discourage it, often describing it pejoratively with words such as "wool gathering," "dreaming," or "fantasizing." By the time most of us enter adolescence, this precious faculty has already atrophied. The relatively few people—well under 10 percent of the population, I should think—who reach adulthood with their ability to make creative use of subjective imagination still intact are often very successful in life, sometimes in business, sometimes in the arts and professions. They are also the people who cannot walk across the plank of wood when it is 2 or 3 feet off the floor. But whatever else they may be, they are all remarkably lucky.

When I explained how you use Psychofeedback every day, my examples were mundane, routine, and easily achieved merely by using your imagination objectively. But let us return for a moment to the bioelectrical hand. If the amputee still has muscles in his forearm, it is sufficient that he, too, uses his imagination objectively to generate the necessary electrical signal which switches the drive motor to forward or reverse. However, when the muscles on the forearm of an amputee are wasted to the extent that he can no longer generate a big enough electrical signal for amplification, he can be trained to use other muscles in his anatomy including the muscles in the trunk. But what is it that has to be trained? *It is his imagination.* It is impossible for him to use other muscles in his anatomy unless he uses his imagination subjectively.

When individuals have to use the electro-mechanical devices and apply the biofeedback therapeutic techniques for the treatment of disorders, it is the imagination which has to be trained and the more complex the debility, the greater the switch from objective to subjective imagining that is required. The patient who is being treated for an allergic reaction to cats, which produces asthma attacks, cannot bring on an attack just by looking at pictures of cats. However, when her imagination has been trained, and she uses it subjectively, then, when she looks at pictures of cats it seems to her that the cats are *actually* with her and an asthmatic attack is triggered which she can then learn to control. Similarly, with the biofeedback machine techniques which have been developed for the control of migraine headache— that of warming the hand by switching the flow of blood from the head to the hand—the individual *must* be able to use his or her imagination subjectively in order to succeed. The more difficult the goal, the *greater* is the necessity for the imagination to be used subjectively.

The power of the subjective imagination is truly prodigious.

Now, the important thing for you to realize is that, even though you may long ago have been brainwashed into thinking your imaginative faculties are mostly useless or even counterproductive, and even though you have allowed these faculties to fall into disuse, *you still have them,* and with a little effort you can learn how to use them again.

And—indeed—you must!

If you do not, you will never be able to make full use of your Psychofeedback mechanism, and you certainly will not be able to achieve the highest and most difficult goals you have set for yourself.

Let me briefly summarize the points I have been trying to make so far about the importance of the imagination. The biocomputer cannot tell the difference between real and imagined experience. When willpower and imagination conflict, imagination will win. Subjective imagination is our most effective means of controlling positive Input into our biocomputers because, under certain conditions, our biocomputers will accept this imaginative Input as "real"; it will become Permanent Storage. And from this storage will come Output—strongly augmented Output—of almost unbelievable power.

Are there other reasons why the subjective imagination is so important in processing Input (thoughts) into the biocomputer? Is there something inherent in the structure of our brains that makes them particularly responsive to this kind of Input?

The answer to this last question is a definite *Yes.* Not only has modern science verified the special receptivity of the brain to imaginative Input, it has even gone a long way toward locating the specific parts of the brain concerned with processing this kind of information. The story of how these discoveries were made is, to my mind, one of the most exciting chapters in the history of self-knowledge.

The central figure in this story is Dr. Roger Sperry, the great psycho-biologist at the California Institute of Technology. Having first made the important discovery that neuron fibers could regenerate and find their way, very precisely, back to the place where they should be connected, Dr. Sperry's next concern was to find out how the mechanism of visual perception worked and how the information was stored in the brain.

The brains of all mammals are divided into two hemispheres. The right hemisphere controls the left side of the body and vice versa. The two hemispheres of the brain are joined together by a structure called the corpus callosum. Until fairly recently it was believed to serve no useful function, but in the early 1950's Dr. Ronald Myers found while doing his doctoral work with Roger Sperry, that the purpose of the corpus callosum was to act as the bridge between the two hemispheres enabling the cross communication of information to be transmitted from one to the other.

When the corpus callosum is surgically divided, neither hemisphere knows what is going on in the other hemisphere. Split-brain cats and monkeys behaved as if each hemisphere had a separate domain of conscious-ness. Extension of these findings to the human brain became possible after two Los Angeles neurosurgeons, Drs. Philip Vogel and Joseph Bogen, had had lengthy discussions with Sperry on the possibility of applying the same surgical procedure as a "last resort" cure of a pa-tient suffering from life-threatening epilepsy. In 1961 they performed such an operation successfully.

To test for hemispheric differences in man, Sperry and Bogen invited a graduate student, Michael Gazza-niga, to join them, and he has continued to work exten-sively in this field.

It was already known that the corpus callosum can be bisected and yet leave no discernible impairment of the faculties, even to the trained observer. Speech, verbal intelligence and reasoning, calculation, movement coor-dination, recall, personality, and temperament are all preserved, even when the hemispheres are no longer connected by the corpus callosum. But what was dis-

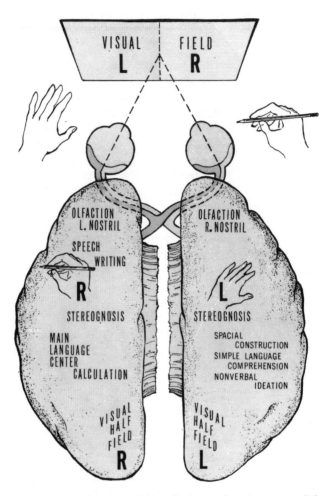

Fig. 7 Schematic drawing of the split brain showing some of the properties of each hemisphere (*illustration by R. W. Sperry*)

covered by Drs. Sperry, Bogen, Gazzaniga and Jerre Levy, whom Sperry credits with being the first to obtain convincing evidence of different cognitive processing of information in the two hemispheres, is—and I choose the words carefully—*utterly amazing.*

It had previously been understood that one brain hemisphere is usually dominant and the other subordinate. The dominant hemisphere is usually the left one,

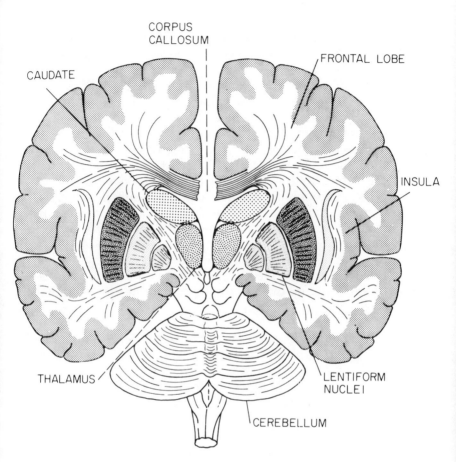

Fig. 8 Side-to-side cross-section of the brain showing the location of the corpus callosum (*illustration by R. W. Sperry*)

and it contains the speech mechanism. Even the majority of left-handed people have their speech mechanism in the left hemisphere. But now, by repeated testing with a number of people and by using a wide range of testing techniques, the investigators found something quite un-

*From *Neuroscience, Third Study Program,* Schmitt and Worden, MIT Press, 1973.

expected. It is not merely a matter of dominance: The two hemispheres use completely different ways to arrive at a solution to a test problem!

What all the tests on people with split brains showed was that the so-called minor hemisphere is, in fact, *the dominant hemisphere in many functions.* The left hemisphere tends to be verbal and mathematical. It processes information in an analytical manner, using symbolic and sequential logic. The right hemisphere, on the other hand, synthesises and perceives on a Gestalt basis. Although not mathematical, it is superior at drawing geometric figures and, in fact, is the half of the brain which is primarily concerned with the mechanism of imagery.

In 1973, for his achievement in medical science, Roger Sperry received the 29th annual Passano Foundation Award and this is what he said at the dinner on that occasion:

> *The findings on hemispheric specialization tell us that our education system and modern society generally, with its very heavy emphasis on communication and on early training in the three R's, discriminates against one whole half of the brain. I refer, of course, to the nonverbal, non-mathematical, minor hemisphere, which we find has its own perceptual, mechanical, and spatial mode of apprehension and reasoning. In our present school system, the minor hemisphere of the brain gets only the barest minimum of formal training, essentially nothing compared to the things that we do to train the left hemisphere.*

I cannot help wondering why nothing has ever been done by the authorities to correct this imbalance. Billions of dollars, yours and mine, are spent each year on research grants and, occasionally, we even hear that we will benefit in some way. Yet I have not been able to find that anything has been done to correct the lamentable state of affairs referred to by Sperry although it would be so easy to insert into the school curriculum, a one hour program each week to give the right side of the brain some exercise and training.

But setting aside the important social implications of these discoveries, what do they mean to you and me individually? Sperry and his colleagues showed that an entire hemisphere of the brain operates in ways that were previously unexpected. Not only is this imagistic, nonverbal, nonmathematical, nonlinear right hemisphere always dominant in the performance of some functions, there appear to be times when it dominates our behavior as a whole.

We have already seen how important it is to control the Input that goes into our biocomputers—how dangerous, for example, an uncontrolled play of the imagination can be. The very fact that our brains are composed of two hemispheres, which operate on different principles, suggests that the problem of controlling Input cannot be altogether simple. For example, control over verbal Input would be much more important for the left hemisphere than for the right; but with respect to an Input consisting mostly of images, the situation would be reversed.

It is no use trying to insert just any old message into a mechanical computer. Unless the message is specially adapted to the computer's capabilities and is then put into the particular language and form the computer is designed to handle, the machine will process the information inefficiently, incorrectly, or not at all.

The same is true of our biocomputers. When we want to insert a thought formula into our Permanent Storage, we have to do it in a way that is compatible with the unique design of the biocomputer: Otherwise, it just won't "take." By the same token, once we know the technique—the proper "code," if you will—for composing messages that the biocomputer will accept into Permanent Storage, we can go beyond mere generalized positive thinking. We can *program* the biocomputer to achieve any number of highly specific goals and can thus attain an almost limitless mastery over ourselves and our environment.

Obviously, this whole matter of control—what it is and how it is exercised—is central to the subject of this book. In all the previous pages I have had to rely heavily on the findings of others, but in this matter I can claim personal expertise. I am referring to my twenty-odd years of experience with the subject of hypnosis.

I might note here that since TM came into prominence in the 1960's, the proponents of hypnosis have levelled accusations against the TM people to the effect that the TM instructors are actually using hypnosis but substituting the euphemism "meditation." I confess that, until 1977, I supported this accusation. The TM instructors have always vigorously denied this allegation and they were right to do so. But whether or not they knew *why* they were correct in their denial, in view of their lack of understanding of the mechanism, is doubtful.

What led me to see the error of my opinion was the realization that there is no such thing as "self-hypnosis." I did not arrive at this conclusion lightly or casually. I did so only after a two year period of deep cogitation. I think you will understand my reluctance to admit that for nearly twenty years I had been making a mistake.

I have no doubt that this statement will provoke controversy. Those who are teaching so-called "self-hypnosis" will accuse me of splitting hairs, playing with words and making semantics serve my purpose. Most definitely, I am not.

There is hypnosis . . . period. When a person has been hypnotized he has agreed to surrender a *measure* of his sovereignty, *some* of his self-control, to the hypnotist. Now, it is impossible for a person to do on his own a number of things which he can do with me in a state of hypnosis. How, then, can you call what a person can do on his own by the same name? It cannot be so.

I have often wondered who originated the familiar statement "all hypnosis is self-hypnosis." Nothing could be further from the truth. There is no doubt in my mind that whoever originated the idea of "self-hypnosis" did so to facilitate the use of hypnosis with people who would otherwise not allow themselves to be hypnotized because of their fear of the phenomenon—i.e., because of negative conceptual storage in their biocomputers relative to hypnosis. It is very difficult to hypnotize a person who has said, even mentally, that he will not be hypnotized. Thus hypnotists who do not have sufficient confidence in their ability or do not have the time or inclination to establish the necessary rapport with the subject find it easier to euphemize: "I'm not going to do anything to you: You will be doing everything yourself, because all hypnosis is self-hypnosis." I have never, under any circumstance, used this sleight of hand procedure, and you can take it from me that no experienced hypnotist believes this.

There is another misstatement that is constantly being made and which I must explain if you are to have a full understanding of the things I will be asking you to do presently. The statement is that "not everyone can be hypnotized." There is no subterfuge here. This is a genuine, even though mistaken, belief held by a number of serious and reputable investigators. The conclusion originates from two different sources. First, the use of hypnosis by the medical profession for therapeutic purposes, and second, the investigation of hypnosis and hypnotic phenomena, usually by psychologists, under so-called "laboratory" conditions, from which come conclusions which are said to have been arrived at "scientifically." I must point out to the investigators, who are sincere and thoughtful men, that I really cannot see anything very scientific about conclusions arrived at which, as the literature indicates, have blandly ignored three critical aspects of hypnosis: *time, technique,* and *technical expertise.* Time means the *number of times* people are taken into hypnosis. Technique means the particular *method used* by the hypnotist. And technical expertise refers to the *degree of proficiency* of the hypnotist.

My own environment for the use of hypnosis was the classroom—a much better environment, I believe, than a physician's office or a research laboratory. And certainly whenever I practiced hypnosis, I always paid the strictest attention to the three critical requirements listed above. Let me try to give you some idea of what these classroom sessions were like.

A typical class consisted of from ten to forty people. At the first lesson the students were given a detailed explanation of hypnosis with much more emphasis as to *what it is not* than what it is. I then explained the method I would use of taking them into hypnosis by carefully worded systematic relaxation, and I further explained that it would be some time before they would recognize that they were, indeed, in a state of hypnosis.

They were told that at each of the eight lessons in the classroom, they would be taken into hypnosis two times. In addition, at each lesson they would be given a different 15-minute cassette tape, the first to be superseded by the second, the second by the third, and so on. They were asked to use the cassette outside the classroom twice each day for the first week and then once every day thereafter until the end of the course. Having my voice on tape is exactly the same as being with me in person, so that it meant that, by the end of the second lesson they had been hypnotized eighteen times, by the end of the third lesson, twenty-seven times; fourth lesson, thirty-six; fifth lesson, forty-five; and so on.

When did these people recognize that they had been taken into a state of hypnosis? The percentage rate of recognition was never less than the following: at the fourth lesson, only 30 percent could answer "yes" to the question: "How many of you know that you have been hypnotized?" At the fifth, 50 percent; at the sixth, about 90 percent. It was only one in one hundred—1 percent— who had not recognized hypnosis by the end of the eighth lesson, which is not at all the same thing as saying they had not been hypnotized. There are characteristics which manifest themselves on the part of a person in hypnosis which are easily discernible, all of which were present even with these people. I would like you to keep in mind, that these results were obtained from hundreds of classes of both sexes ranging in age from 14 to 83!

These statements can very easily be verified, as they were by Captain Richard Sandstrom,* head of the Los Angeles Police Department Hypnosis Squad.

Ever since the discovery of hypnosis in the early 1800's there have been two persistent notions which are still with us but should be dropped immediately. The first is the notion that one person can do something to another person which can only be described as "instant" hypnosis. The second notion is that there are a variety of techniques which can be used to take a person into hypnosis. These two notions are effective and applicable to only a *minority* of the population. They are not effective with the majority, with the inevitable result of failure by practitioners to hypnotize these people, and this has led to the false belief that not everyone can be hypnotized.

I am convinced that it is this fallacy that, for nearly two centuries, has prevented us from understanding a *very profound and important mechanism.*

It is quite clear that a person must *learn* to be hypnotized, and providing the three T's, time, technique,

---

*Capt. Sandstrom and the Squad had been trained as hypnotists by people, understood to be experts, who also had said that not everyone could be hypnotized. The Captain found out this was not true.

and technical expertise are meticulously attended to, everyone can learn to be hypnotized.

But what is it exactly that a person who wants to get more living out of life must learn? Merely to say, you can learn to be hypnotized does not provide you with knowledge, which, perhaps, you did not possess previously. And yet to understand your own brain mechanisms and the concept I will put before you in a moment, you must know exactly what has to be learned by the individual who is to be hypnotized.

Let me remind you that one of the functions of your Reticular Activating System is to analyze incoming information, and either to accept and pass through relevant information to your biocomputer or *to reject it and not pass it through.* When a person has been hypnotized that function is inhibited, *it is negated;* never completely negated, of course, but the degree of negation need not concern us here. The biocomputer—that part of the brain which functions at the unconscious level—cannot and must not have the ability to reject. If it did there would be utter chaos and nothing would ever get done. Imagine the situation that would exist if I passed through the information "I'm going to take a drink of coffee," to my biocomputer and it decided, "No, you're not." "Yes, I am." "No, you're not." "Yes, I am." I would be unable to function.

If I were with you now, and if I said to you, "You have forgotten your name," you would think I was trying to play some kind of a game with you. You would probably smile and say "Oh, have I?" But the fourth or fifth time that I said it, you would become serious and respond with a "Don't be ridiculous" kind of statement, and to put an end to something so stupid, you would probably add, "My name is John Doe" or whatever it is. Your RAS would have analyzed the information "You have forgotten your name" each time and would have rejected it.

If, however, you were in a state of hypnosis and I said "You have forgotten your name, what is it?" You might try as hard as possible to remember, but you would be *unable to remember your own name!* How can anyone forget his own name? Only if the analytical function of the RAS has been bypassed and the information gets into the biocomputer which *must act upon the information as though it was so,* "You have forgotten your name," would become a fact.

Occasionally I have helped a student to stop smoking by using hypnosis. After they have been hypnotized, they are told that shortly they will light a cigarette, but that the cigarette will have the vilest, most horrible taste. That with each successive draw of smoke from the cigarette, the taste will become more vile and that they will be forced to extinguish the cigarette after the third inhalation. When this happens, there is utter amazement on their part. Since they became hooked, cigarettes have always tasted delicious. How can this happen? Only if the analytical function of the RAS has been negated and the information, "Cigarette tastes vile," gets into the biocomputer, which *must act on that information as though it were so,* then "Cigarette tastes vile" becomes a fact.

Obviously, therefore, what has to be learned is the surrendering to the hypnotist of the control, analytical function of the RAS. But, and this is the important matter for you to understand, contrary to popular belief an individual does not need to be hypnotized to learn how to use this mechanism.

If we accept that everyone can be hypnotized instead of the contrary, then it means that everyone is fitted with this mechanism. This is what I meant when I said previously that the fallacy, that not everyone could be hypnotized, has prevented us from understanding for nearly two centuries a very profound and important mechanism.

It is apparent that as the evolutionary process was taking place millions of years ago, while the cortex was developing, the Reticular Activating System was also changing and developing as it made all the new synaptic connections. This process equipped us with our imagination and our Psychofeedback mechanism, thereby enabling us to achieve a higher order of goal seeking that was not dependent on our past performance, as it is in every other species. It is also apparent that the same evolutionary process also equipped us with an additional mechanism whereby the analytical function of our RAS can be deactivated, thereby allowing us direct access to our biocomputer and giving us the opportunity of ensuring that the best possible program is contained therein.

This last concept is perfectly consistent and harmonious with the concepts embodied in Cybernetics, those of *control* and communication. It is also harmonious with the cybernetic definition of Motivation, i.e., the energizing and *control* of purposeful behavior toward specific goals. And since this concept requires a name, I shall call it Reticular Activating System Control, or, for short, RASCON.

When we realize that each of us is equipped with this mechanism and that we can learn to deactivate and reactivate it as we desire, having learned to do so, we truly become the masters of our lives and our destinies.

We all know that our personalities are made up of a number of characteristics, and we all know that if we are to obtain the bounties of our society, the positive characteristics have to be dominant. Many people feel helpless as they struggle to eliminate those characteristics which prevent them from reaping the rewards of their efforts. Yet if we accept the fact that we can change existing programs and insert new ones—for example, exchange a "procrastination" program for a "do-it-now" program—simply by using RASCON, we will have taken the first step toward learning one of the most exciting things that can happen to a person.

It is quite apparent that something like RASCON

has been known, albeit intuitively, by Eastern cultures for centuries. But not being able to explain the source of this inner power rationally is probably the reason why it is rooted deeply in mysticism and religion. To unsophisticated people, anything which could produce such marvelous feats of mind over matter had to be a special gift from a deity and only be used in the glorification of that deity.

Similarly, the Transcendental Meditation people have been practicing a form of RASCON without fully understanding what they were doing and, in consequence, with some undesirable results. The psychophysiological ritual taught by the TM people does trigger the deactivating mechanism of the RAS, eliminating the analytical function. What I feel the TM people have failed to realize is that the mechanism must be *reactivated* and returned to its everyday routine analytical function, and this must be done *deliberately*. When the Reticular Activating System is deliberately deactivated, it must be *deliberately* reactivated, otherwise *it will remain* in the deactivated state.

The students of meditation are instructed to clear their mind of all purposeful thoughts by concentrating on the so-called mantra for twenty minutes, twice a day. The meditation instructor will say you will be able to do so after being taught their technique. I say you will not be able to do so. Furthermore until Input (thought) is linked to a goal (purpose) there can be no intelligent accomplishment. However, the instructors also tell you, just as Herbert Benson does in *The Relaxation Response,* that you need not be concerned if *other thoughts* should come into your mind. But anyone who understands the power of thought, unmediated by the analytical and judgmental faculties of the RAS, will see that these *other thoughts* can be a matter of very great concern indeed!

An example of my own acquaintance is Larry Griffith, the owner of Griffith & Co., printers and lithographers in Los Angeles, who do all my printing. Larry is a successful businessman, but he has had to work at it. He told me that, by nature, he is a slob (his word, which surprised me because he always looks immaculate) and that he has always had to be strict with himself and control his natural desires. He started with a TM class because he had heard so many beneficial things about meditating. The day after the first lesson, Larry found he had to struggle to get out of bed. He couldn't be bothered to shower and shave. All he wanted to do was get a few cans of beer and some peanuts and crackers and get comfortable in front of the TV, which was his Sunday treat to himself. *But this was Tuesday!*

This state of affairs lasted until Larry realized that the only thing different in his life was the meditating that he was doing for twenty minutes, twice a day. As soon as he realized this, he stopped meditating, but it took a day before he was back to his usual hustling self.

Through meditation Larry had succeeded in deactivating his RAS, but he had not taken the crucial next step. Instead of inserting a useful, carefully constructed program into his biocomputer, he allowed random, self-indulgent, and generally purposeless thoughts to slip into his biocomputer. Bad Input results in bad Output, and Larry suddenly found himself coping with life in a way that was for him disastrous.

If, by any chance, you have had a similar experience, you can consider yourself fortunate in at least one respect. It is an indication that you may be able to deactivate your RAS more quickly than most people. And as you will see from the instructions I shall soon be giving you, that can be an enormous asset.

Am I going to ask you to meditate? I most certainly am not. What I am going to teach you is the antithesis, the exact opposite, of what is taught by schools of meditation.

As I have already explained, I decided in 1977 that there could be no such thing as self- or autohypnosis. Up to that time my students had been learning how to deactivate their RAS while under the impression that they were learning autohypnosis, and they had all succeeded in doing this very successfully. Yet it was becoming quite obvious to me that what was important here was not hypnosis, as such, but the psychophysiological technique which was used in the learning process. This was the key to controlling the RAS.

I was also sure that individuals *had to be told* that they were going to be taken into hypnosis; otherwise *the same technique* could be used and *they would not go into hypnosis,* and this has proved to be correct.

It may interest you to know what has transpired in the classes since I abandoned autohypnosis and replaced it with RASCON. At the first lesson of every class which has been started since that time, the subject of hypnosis and hypnotic phenomena has been discussed in much the same manner as we have discussed it in this book. I explain to the class that the psychophysiological technique I intend to teach is the same as that used to effect hypnosis, but that in this case hypnosis will not be the result. Later on in the course, just to make sure the difference is clear to everyone, I suggest that two or three people volunteer to be taken into hypnosis and afterward tell the entire class if what they experienced in hypnosis was the same as what they experienced using RASCON. Typical responses have been;

"I couldn't think—it seemed as if I was in suspended animation."

"I felt very resentful because I knew I couldn't do anything."

"Completely different. I tried to make myself comfortable and found I couldn't move."

No, RASCON is decidedly *not* meditation and *not* hypnosis, auto- or otherwise. What is it, then? We shall find out shortly, but first let us turn to the heart of the matter and consider the question of goals.

7 Goals

Among other utterly fallacious pronouncements made by Sigmund Freud was his attempt to explain human conduct in terms of "drives." It is absolutely certain that goals are a vastly more important aspect of human behavior than so-called "drives." I am sure that many people who believe they need psychotherapy do so as a result of never having been educated about the necessity of establishing realistic goals for themselves.

Running and jogging became popular in 1976-78 as a rapidly increasing pursuit of millions of Americans, all of whom started as a result of wanting to stay in good shape. Some journalists, writing about the phenomenon, have not been able to understand the attraction; particularly when the runners and joggers said they felt so good about their activities and yet could not explain why they felt this way. Yet, if we accept the cybernetic interpretation of human behavior, the explanation is very simple. Joggers are forever in quest of better performance, of running farther or faster or more effortlessly. In short, they are constantly setting goals for themselves.

And why does this make them feel good? Because in setting and pursuing goals, they are doing what they were designed to do. Alone among animals, man is a goal setter. The entire evolution of his brain and nervous system has been oriented to this end. The biocomputer literally *demands* goals and is actually unhappy when it does not have them.

To be sure, the biocomputer is no more discriminating about the intrinsic worth of goals than a mechanical computer is about the worth of the programs it is fed. Tell the biocomputer that your goal is simply to exist, and it will help you to do just that. It will not tell you that simply existing is not much of a goal.

But if neither bio- nor mechanical computers are much concerned about the worth of the goals presented to them, they are extraordinarily finicky about the manner of presentation. If a mechanical computer cannot receive or understand Input, it cannot process it. Neither can a biocomputer.

Let me give you an example.

Hold a pen between your thumb and forefinger, keeping the other three fingers out of the way. Keep your forefinger horizontal. Hold the pen or pencil firmly, look at the end of the pen or pencil, and, without taking your eyes off the end of the pen, say to yourself and *think* hard—I am emphasizing the word *think* because everyone knows that someone can say something and think exactly the opposite—"I can drop it, I can drop it, I can drop it, I can drop it, I can drop it." Repeat that over and over to yourself fairly quickly and *while you are doing that*—while you are *thinking and* talking to yourself—try to open your thumb and forefinger.

If you did as I asked, the pen did not drop. If it did,

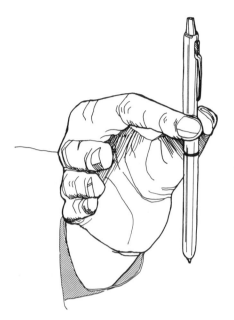

Fig. 9 Relative position of fingers and pen

you did not follow my instructions precisely. Do it again after you have read the explanation of the mechanics which are involved.

First, you must understand that responsibility for every physical movement that you make has been delegated to your biocomputer. Unless we deliberately think about it, there is not one joint that we move, muscle that we activate, that we control at the conscious level. Reach out with your right hand and turn the page of the book and then turn it back again. Were you thinking consciously *how* to stretch out your arm and hand, *how* to manipulate your fingers into the hooking position when you turned the page? Of course you were not.

One of the concepts that I have gone to some length to get across to you is the notion of "control," which is fundamental to the entire science of Cybernetics, particularly control of information.

Wiener also showed a great concern for this matter, particularly in the very practical matter of the *loss of value* or quality of the information resulting in the transmission of that information, regardless of the method of transmission and reception of the information.

In *The Human Use of Human Beings,** Wiener arrives at conclusions on these matters.

A number of times I have asked you to read Wiener's words and I have said that his conclusions were of vital importance. It is impossible to categorize one thing as being more important than another thing; even so, I am going to say that nothing he said is more important than the following:

> Semantically significant *[emphasis mine] information, in man as well as in the machine, is information which* gets through *[emphasis mine] to an activating mechanism in the system that receives it, despite man's and/or nature's attempts to subvert it. From the point of view of Cybernetics, semantics defines the extent of meaning and controls its loss in a communications system.*

I want to come back to this very important statement presently, but for the moment let us return to the question of the pen that would not drop.

Why didn't the pen drop? As usual, the answer has to do with Cybernetics. Every human being is a semantic transmitting and receiving apparatus. Semantics are the "codes" in which we send, receive, and process information. The words that you are reading on this page are semantics, I am transmitting my semantics—this information—to you with pen and paper, and you are receiving my semantics, with your eyes. If I were speaking with you person-to-person, I would be transmitting my semantics to you with my mouth and vocal cords, and

---

*By Norbert Wiener. Copyright 1950, 1954 by Norbert Wiener. Reprinted by permission of Houghton Mifflin Company.

you would be receiving my semantics with your ears. If I were speaking to you in sign language, I would transmit with my hands and you would receive with your eyes. And so on.

When you held the pen, what was the information that you passed through to your biocomputer? The information was "I *can* drop it." But "I *can* drop it" is not semantically significant information for the purpose of getting through and activating the mechanism of your finger and thumb. As you passed through the information "I can drop it," your biocomputer just stood by and said "Okay, Okay, Okay, Standing By, Standing By, Standing By." For the purpose of opening your finger and thumb, the semantically significant information would be "I drop it." The word "can" converts the reality into a mere possibility.

In terms of goal setting, the implications of this demonstration are fairly obvious. Information destined for the biocomputer has to be phrased with absolute precision if it is to be acted upon. And in order to ensure this precision, *it should always be written down* clearly, concisely, and without ambiguity. Possibly you may have read some so-called behavior-modification books on how to quit smoking or how to lose weight that advised you to write down your resolutions. You may have thought the advice unnecessary. In any case, I doubt you were given any good reason for doing so, since it is unlikely that the authors themselves understood *why* the advice was essential. But now you know the reason.

Such goals as "I want to be financially independent" or "I want a promotion," while they seem clear and concise, are not sufficient for the biocomputer to act upon efficiently. The biocomputer must have more precise information.

The majority of corporations set quotas for their sales staffs. They tell their sales personnel that they expect them to sell a certain amount of product or service within a given period of time—usually per year. This is, of course, cybernetically correct—which is excellent as far as it goes. But it does not go far enough.

Salespeople should not only be told what is expected of them in volume, they should also be given some indication of how they can achieve their quotas, their goal. I am not referring to selling skills or the number of calls or the number of presentations they need to make to reach their quota. Calls and presentations are merely the nuts and bolts of the business of selling and very often take care of themselves. Rather, the "how" should be implicit in the precision with which the goal is stated.

As you know, classes are conducted at the corporate level, and the majority of my students are sales professionals who, because they are working on a commission basis, have the opportunity to increase their income very substantially. During the lesson dealing with goals and the semantics of goals, all my students jot down the exact words of a "goal contract" on scratch paper. They are then asked to either print or type the goal onto a card of manageable size and bring it to the next lesson, *memorized*. They must show it to me, and they must show me that they have memorized it by reciting it in class.

If you are a salesperson, I ask you also to copy the goal contract shown here without changing it in any way.

To begin with, it is preferable that you set only a one-year goal for yourself. I realize that this is not a very long-term goal, but is better for you until you have become truly goal-oriented.* It need not be exactly one year;

---

*Of course, if you are already goal oriented, there is no reason why you should not set a much longer goal for yourself—say, five, ten, or even twenty years. In fact, if your goal is to become financially independent, it must be so. Financial independence: to have earned an amount of money which will earn an amount of money which will keep you in the manner that you demand.

Goal Contract

Date _____

By_____ I will have earned a minimum of

$_____

I will have earned this amount as a result of giving the most efficient service of which I am capable, rendering the fullest possible quantity and the best possible quality of service in the capacity of

_____

This is an irrevocable contract I make with myself.

Signed _____

Witnessed _____

Fig. 10 Sample form for the Financial Goal Contract which you should copy, paste onto a card, and always carry with you.

perhaps you and your corporation have a particular financial accounting period that you want to work with. But whatever the period, *you must put down the date explicitly.*

Your career goal as a salesperson must surely be to earn more money. (Can it be otherwise?) So what amount should you shoot for? This is dependent on some variables. The biggest variable, of course, is your intensity of purpose; the others are how long you have been in sales and what it is that you are selling.

So you must pick a figure that is realistic, given the variables. I want you to set a very high financial goal for yourself, but *it must not be a fantasy figure.* Always keeping in mind that exactly the same effort is required to aim high as to aim low, you should set a goal, which, when you look at it, will leave you somewhat incredulous, doubting your ability.

Yet you should not be concerned, at the moment, about how this is going to happen. When the goal contract becomes part of the Permanent Storage in your biocomputer, when you use Psychofeedback in the way you are supposed to use it, then like any other goal seeking, servo mechanism, your biocomputer will find the way to take you to the goal. Zigging and zagging to be sure, but all the time directing your every move, acting upon the information you put into it.

All of my students were once in the position which you are probably now in, wondering if what I was telling them was correct. You have heard about some of them already, but I think you should hear about some others. I have selected three from different companies in the insurance industry.

Toward the end of 1972, I taught the course to a class at the Santa Monica branch of the Prudential Insurance Company. During the lesson on goal setting, I pointed out that it would not be unrealistic for most of the class to think in terms of doubling their production in 1973.

After the lesson, a man named Lester Martin and I had a chat. Lester told me that it was impossible for him to do that which I asked the class to do—i.e., double his production. He went on to explain that he was in a unique position. Although he was on the staff of the Santa Monica branch, he had his own office at the Western Regional Office and he handled solely the insurance needs of the employees of Prudential. He was, so to speak, the "insurance men's insurance man."

I said, "Lester, you wouldn't mind earning $5,000 more in 1973, would you?"

"Of course not," he said, "but it just isn't there. I know the potential of my position, so how can I expect more."

"Lester, in class I asked you not to be concerned for the moment about how this was going to happen. Now will you do something for me? Put down a figure in your goal contract which will increase your income by $5,000 in 1973."

When he said he would, it was with the air of someone humoring a half-wit.

I subsequently discovered that Lester was a veteran who had been selling insurance at Prudential for twenty-two years. Every year Lester wrote a million dollars of insurance, but every year he would go right down to the wire—the month of December—before he finally did it. What has happened since then is a matter of record.

In 1973 he wrote over $1,000,000 of insurance by the beginning of August and went on to total $1,600,000 for the year. In 1974 he wrote $2,000,000, with $34,000 premiums. In 1975 he wrote $3,256,000 with $70,640 premiums. In 1976; $3,372,000, with $78,000 premiums. In 1977, although he only worked ten months, he wrote $2,765,000 with $74,349 premiums. This was the man who said he had reached his maximum in 1972.

Steven Douglass, who is with The Travelers Insurance Companies, was a student in October 1973. At twenty eight years of age he was doing quite well, holding a position designated Agency Manager, in which he was responsible for the training of rookie insurance agents.

Steve set himself two career goals in 1973. He wanted to pass all the examinations leading to his CLU before he was thirty two, i.e., to do in four years something which normally takes six years; and he wanted to become the youngest ever branch manager of The Travelers. He knew that the only way to the second of these was via the regional office, so he made that his immediate goal.

In June 1974 Steve was promoted to regional manpower consultant. In July 1977 he was again promoted, to branch manager in Phoenix, Arizona. He was not the youngest ever; somebody beat him by two months! But he earned his certification at thirty-two in 1978!

When Steve set these goals in 1974, he really did not think they were possible, as he is the first to admit. Yet, by using RASCON and Psychofeedback, as they are supposed to be used, he did so.

His next goal of taking Arizona to $100 million of production in four years will also be achieved because he continues to use these powerful brain mechanisms. He is getting everyone else in his branch to use them also.

Lester Martin and Steve Douglass were already doing quite well before they learned the importance of using semantically significant information in their goal contracts. Does the same thing happen with a person who has not been doing well?

Karen Cleaver of New York Life Insurance Company was one of those people when she became a student in 1977. She had been an insurance salesperson for eigh- teen months and was barely surviving, earning around $1,000 per month. The one-year goal she set for herself was $30,000. She earned $50,000! She was the first woman to make New York Life's Presidents' Council in the southern California region, and the first agent, man or woman, to be so honored in her General Office. She reset her goals and became the leading woman agent in the region and a qualifying member of the prestigious.

industry-wide Million Dollar Round Table.

Although we have been talking exclusively about salesmen up to now, goal contracts are by no means confined to increasing sales performance or personal income. Dr. Arthur Muir is a brilliant young physicist with Rockwell International. When Art contacted me in the fall of 1972 it was because some of his friends had told him about the course. After the first lesson, he and I had a conversation in which he explained his reasons for wanting to become a student. He had had a job in Rockwell's California corporate office for four years. He explained that he had never expected to hold the post for that long, and he believed that he had been passed over for promotion because he was not sufficiently outgoing. When I asked him what direction he would like to see his career take, he said he would really like to get a management position at Rockwell's Science Center at Thousand Oaks, California. I told him that when we got to the goal-setting lesson, he should incorporate both his personality goal and his career goal into his goal contract.

Nine months after completing the program, Art was transferred to the Science Center as group leader, heading a team of six other scientists. Only nine months later, he was promoted to director of the Physics and Chemistry Department, leading a team of forty scientists. In 1975 he was given the task of coordinating all the Science Center activities with the many Rockwell commercial divisions and with national universities. It is understood that such a position calls for a person with considerable charm and a very outgoing personality.

You may have wondered how Art's personality goal was included within dates. It wasn't. Although specific dates are always desirable in goal setting, some contracts will not have a specific date by which the goal is to be accomplished. The reason for that, very simply, is that those objectives for which the individuals are striving are ongoing. They seek those objectives now and forever. If you are setting similar goals for yourself, you, too, should start your goal contract with the words "Forthwith and for the foreseeable future—"

In addition to highly specific information about the goals in question, every goal contract must contain the following phraseology:

> *... As a result of giving the most efficient service of which I am capable, rendering the fullest possible quantity, and the best possible quality of service.*

I urge you—no, I do more than that, I beg and beseech you—not to be afraid of those words. You may say, "But I already give the most efficient service of which I'm capable, and I always render it in the fullest possible quantity, and I never think of anything less than the best possible quality." Fine. *Nevertheless, you must not only include these words, you must memorize them as well as you remember your own name.*

Unfortunately, your biocomputer may already contain more programs tending toward procrastination, laziness, or second-rate performance than you are aware of. Should this be the case, the formula I have just given you could be a crucial piece of counterprogramming. Please do not fail to use it.

All of which prompts me to a brief digression, for which I ask your indulgence. I write as a guest in your country. A resident alien of Welch parentage brought up in England, I wonder, as I have done so very, very often, if the people of America realize how fortunate they are. I wonder what conceptual storage is in the 220 million biocomputers relative to this country and this society. Do the people of America realize that here, far more than anywhere else in the world, they have something unique? Not only do you have a democracy but you also have something which is perhaps more important: *a meritocracy.*

For the people who are diligent, who show that they *merit* them, this society has bountiful rewards. Yet I see a pervasive and very infectious habit of doing as little as possible and taking as much as possible spreading like a virus through society, ironically, nowhere more than in government offices.

I am not asking you to be altruistic and give without a thought of what you will receive. But if you are to receive, it will only be in return for a service that you have rendered. So commit yourself to giving the most efficient service of which you are capable, rendering the fullest possible quantity and the best possible quality of service. You will find that these words are the *semantically significant information* which will activate the mechanism of your own biocomputer, and take you to whatever goal you set for yourself.

Returning to the broader aspect of Wiener's statement, and keeping in mind that every human being is a semantic (word) transmitting and receiving apparatus, without doubt the wisest piece of advice is to always remember that it is better to wish that you had said something than to wish that *you had not said it*—to choose your words carefully, making sure that when you transmit your information (speak), the receiver of the information (listener) processes the information with the *same* conceptual storage.

Professional salespeople should realize that when they give a presentation they are intending to use semantically significant information (words) which will activate the receiver's (prospect's) mechanism into buying.

One of the reasons why salespeople find telephone prospecting so difficult is because they have not prepared the semantics they are going to transmit with sufficient care. Perhaps it would be fairer to say without sufficient knowledge.

One example should suffice to show what I mean. I get many calls from real estate people searching for listings, and I'm sure that you do also. It isn't necessary to repeat the different sets of semantics which are said to me on the phone. The point is that they have always activated my mechanism into a polite "No, thank you." (It is the long succession of no's which reduce a person's resilience and cause the turnover of manpower in the sales profession.)

If the person calling used semantics similar to the following, "Mr. Thomas, we have a constant demand for property in your area. May I ask you please, is there any chance that you will be selling your property within the next two years?" Providing that the information is transmitted at a slow conversational speed and that there is a brief pause between the three words "next-two-years." By the time the information has been processed conceptually, "next two years" is the distant future. I would probably have to think for a moment and then the chances are that I would say, "Two years? Well I honestly don't know about that" or something similar. Certainly I would be much less likely to say "No." And, if I do not say "No," I have, in fact, started a conversation, which should be the objective of anyone in the real estate business, because that is how they will build a business.

Let us return to the matter at hand, the phraseology of goal contracts. As you read the goals in the following pages, you will see that some of them involve career goals where the individuals are earning fixed salaries. All these individuals have acted on my statement that I hoped that they were ready to commit themselves—in writing—to "giving the most efficient service, etc.," in return for their salary. Occasionally, a student may be diffident about specifically including the exact salary he or she earns. There is nothing wrong with that; but in such cases, I insist that the student include the words: "For the salary I earn, I will give the most efficient service, etc." I avoid the phrase "the money I make"; it is semantically imprecise, only governments, with their mints "make" money!

Quite frequently I am asked if the actual achieving of the goal is important. Of course it is important. But it is *less important* than the actual setting or establishment of the goal. If you do not achieve your goal, you can believe me when I tell you that the strength of character you will have gained in the attempt will better equip you for your next attempt. Even, perhaps, for your *repeated* attempts, if your goal is a particularly high one. But in no case will you be disappointed. Even if you fall short of your goal on your first try, you will nevertheless be amazed at the progress you have made toward reaching it.

Indeed, one of the most interesting immediate results of writing your goal(s) down clearly, concisely, and without ambiguity, and then memorizing them, is that *you will feel better* when you have done so. The reason for this is that, like those joggers we spoke of earlier, you are doing something your biocomputer has been wanting you to do. It is as though the biocomputer heaves a great sigh of relief and says, "At last. Now I know where we are going."

In the next chapter, you will be shown how to start using RASCON. Everytime you do so I want you to spend about two minutes imagining as vividly as you can that *you have already achieved your goal,* using Psychofeedback, inserting into your biocomputer the results of your *present* performance. By selling this volume of business, I will earn this amount of money, and I will be able to do *that*—the things you will do which perhaps you cannot do now, or the things you will own which perhaps you cannot afford now. Savor and enjoy the rewards of achieving your high financial goal, and as you do so generate within yourself a feeling of excitement, of pleasure, and of triumph.

Your goal may not be a financial goal, and yet it must have an end result which is going to give you pleasure, and you must be able to imagine the end result.

Now that I have given you an introduction to the

art and science of drafting goal contracts, I am going to conclude this chapter by giving you a sampling of some fully written-out contracts. Before doing so, however, I want to remind you that accurate contract writing is not the whole story. Still to come is the matter of RASCON— the technique whereby the terms of the contract are actually inserted into the biocomputer.

The contracts that follow are all real, the work of former students, although some of the names have been changed. I have tried to select them in such a way as to illustrate both a variety of goals and variations in phraseology.

GOAL CONTRACT / MARCH 1, 1975

Forthwith and from this day forward, I will strive to advance in the company organization as fast and as far as is humanly possible, be it with Nixdorf or any other company.

I will increase my yearly income by $10,000 in the next three years or less. I will start a savings program and deposit at least $10 per week.

I will start exercising regularly and lose 10 pounds by August 1, 1975, and not gain it back.

I will accomplish these goals as a result of giving the most efficient service of which I am capable, rendering the fullest possible quantity and the best possible quality of service in the capacity of any job title I may ever hold.

This is an irrevocable contract I make with myself.

M. Manter

CAREER GOALS CONTRACT / JULY 3, 1977

By September 1, 1978:
1. I will have seen to it that my materials have been accepted by a publisher;

2. I will be at least half finished preparing them for publication;

3. I will have completed the necessary restructuring of my classes;

4. I will be working on a teacher's guide, tape recordings, or other means of making the classes available to other individuals, institutions, and organizations; and

5. At least 35 new families will have enthusiastically adopted the life-style I teach.

All of this will have been accomplished as a result of my having given the most efficient service of which I am capable, rendering the fullest possible quantity, and the best possible quality of service in the capacities of writer-compiler, course originator, and teacher.

This is an irrevocable contract I make with myself.

Sylvia Rosenberg

Here is a student who set herself a very high career goal. She kept her personal goals separate, they follow.

PERSONAL GOALS CONTRACT / JULY 4, 1977

Beginning today, Monday, July 4, 1977, and for the foreseeable future, my personal goals are:

1. To go to sleep quickly and sleep soundly every night;

2. To set aside a minimum of 15 minutes each day for problem solving and program planning;

3. To be friendly, outgoing, and self-confident, even when I am confronted with negative people and situations;

4. To organize my home life with the same effi-

ciency and enthusiasm I apply to my work;

5. To support my husband and children in their endeavors;

6. To establish and stabilize my weight at a constant 118 pounds; and

7. To relax completely one day each week, without allowing weekday cares to interfere.

I will accomplish my goals:

1. By self-discipline and a "do-it-now" attitude;

2. By working enthusiastically, systematically, and efficiently six days each week; and

3. By using and developing my inherited and acquired abilities to the fullest possible extent.

In accomplishing my goals, I will become a better person, wife, mother, housewife, and teacher.

This is an irrevocable contract I make with myself.

Sylvia Rosenberg

GOAL CONTRACT / APRIL 22, 1974

By June 20, 1976:

1. I will have fashioned my life to that befitting a Christian.

2. I will become a more loyal friend and be less critical of others.

3. I will earn straight "A's" in my last two years of high school.

4. I will become completely organized, overcoming my procrastination, and developing more self-discipline.

5. I will obtain the spot of first trumpet, first chair in the Saxon Concert Band.

I will go about these goals with great vigor and immense dedication. I will give the best quality of service in the capacity of Christian, friend, student, and musician.

This is an irrevocable contract that I make with myself.

Tom Grainger

GOAL CONTRACT / MARCH 10, 1975

Forthwith and for the foreseeable future, I will give the most efficient service of which I am capable, rendering the best possible quality and the fullest possible quantity of service in the capacity of Director of Clinical Rehabilitation Services.

I will be a more confident person and act in a more confident way allowing myself the credit I deserve, while at the same time acknowledging and allowing others theirs.

I will express my feelings and not fear them.

I will be a leader and be self-reliant and also include others in my achievements.

I will no longer fear new experiences, but enjoy and look forward to meeting new people and old friends, doing new things, offering my opinions, giving all types of professional services and presentations in a confident manner.

I will stay on my diet to the best of my ability and avoid foods that are not healthy.

I will exercise regularly.

I will no longer worry about things I cannot control, but will distinguish between constructive planning and dysfunctional worrying.

I will continue to listen to the tape and concentrate on the principles therein.

This is an irrevocable contract that I make with myself.

Martin G. Brodwin

GOAL CONTRACT / JULY 7, 1977

Forthwith and in the foreseeable future I will have obtained the following goals:

1. I will have reached and maintained my goal weight of 120 pounds by August 19, 1977.
2. I will achieve a 4.0 grade point average in all of my classes.
3. I will lead a Christian life in the fullest possible sense.
4. I will become a more fully developed person in every possible way, developing and becoming more confident, more decisive, more determined, more efficient, more organized, more open and honest, more responsible, less inhibited, happier, more energetic, more outgoing, more aware of myself and in control of myself, thereby becoming a more alive, vivacious and totally enthusiastic person.

I will have attained these goals as a result of giving the most efficient service of which I am capable. Rendering the fullest possible quantity and best possible quality of service in the capacity of a student and a person. This is an irrevocable contract I make with myself.

Jill Ward

GOAL CONTRACT / FEBRUARY 21, 1975

By January 1, 1976, I will have earned $14,105. I will have earned this amount as a result of giving the most efficient service of which I am capable, rendering the fullest possible quantity and the best possible quality of service in the capacity of Section Manager, accounting, payroll, call director operators, A/P, Cashiering.

Learning the ins and outs of the P & L in approximately six months to a year.

To promote a person in my section to become a section manager. Prepare Karin Schuler for my job as section manager in one year's time.

To become the best woman administrative manager in two years—beginning of 1977.

Learn company policy extensively this year.

Learn specifics of all administrative jobs in my section this year.

To have 95 percent of all my debts paid off by December 31, 1975.

Achieve 140-143 average in winter bowling league which started in September 1974.

Lose 5-10 pounds and keep the weight off.

Save $1,000 by the end of December 1975.

This is an irrevocable contract I make with myself.

Dee Watkins

GOAL CONTRACT / FEBRUARY 23, 1977

By January 1, 1980, I will have established my own professional office and be conducting a full time business as a Land Surveyor. As the first step toward obtaining this goal, I will as of this date become actively engaged in establishing a part-time business for weekends and holidays so that I may acquaint the area with myself and the professional service that I will provide. By January 1, 1979, I will have obtained all instruments, equipment, and related items needed for my business from fees earned by my part-time business.

Between January 1, 1979, and January 1, 1980, I will have become financially sound and not dependent upon the salary of my present position. This will enable me to make my transition from this position to conducting my own business.

I will have achieved these goals as a result of

giving the most efficient service of which I am capable, rendering the fullest possible quantity and the best possible quality of service in the capacity of Land Surveyor.

This is an irrevocable contract I make with myself.

Bill Williams

GOAL CONTRACT / OCTOBER 26, 1973

As of January 1974 I will put $20 a week into a savings account for the purpose of accruing enough money to resume my education. By approximately September 1975 I will reenter college and work toward and complete a Master's degree. During this period as well as subsequently I shall strive to be a loving mother and wife; keep my temper and sense of humor; feel concern for, and an interest in, those around me. I will use my time wisely, so that I may, in an organized manner, do yard work, keep house and enter into social activities involving my own interests as well as my husband's and children's. At all times I will give the most efficient service of which I am capable, rendering the fullest possible quantity and the best possible quality of service as a wife, mother and student.

This is an irrevocable contract that I make with myself.

Sally Taylor

GOAL CONTRACT / MARCH 3, 1974

Forthwith my goal is to be more self-disciplined, patient, tolerant, and understanding of all people with whom I come into contact, so that each night when I prepare for bed I can look back upon the day and honestly know that I regret only those words left unsaid and those deeds left undone.

I will obtain my real estate license by June 30, 1974, so that I can more fully understand and appreciate my wife's work and be of help to her in achieving her goals.

I will earn $47,000 in my job as a pilot and while doing my work in the most professional manner I will give the most efficient service of which I am capable, rendering the fullest possible quantity and the best possible quality of service.

My wife and I will jointly make investments which will appreciate by $10,000 within one year.

This is an irrevocable contract I make with myself.

Joe Franks

GOAL CONTRACT

Forthwith and in the foreseeable future, in order to attain even greater happiness for myself and for those around me, I will have improved myself in the following ways:

1. I will be punctual for any and all occasions.
2. I will organize my time in order to make the best possible use of every minute in every day.
3. I will make decisions more quickly and decisively.
4. I will keep our home free from unnecessary "clutter" which annoys Jim.
5. I will be more understanding of the *personal* needs of each of our children, and continue to let them know of our constant love and support at *all times*.
6. I will be even more aware of the *needs* and desires of others at all times.
7. I will continue to support, encourage, and help

Jim in his profession and in his life in *every* way I
can.

8. I will no longer be tired in the evenings so I can
give Jim the loving affection he needs at the end of
each day.

I will have improved in each of these ways as a
result of giving the most efficient service of which I
am capable, rendering the fullest possible quantity,
and the best possible quality of service in the capacity of wife, mother, daughter, sister, and friend.

This is an irrevocable contract I make with myself.

Jean Jackson

GOAL CONTRACT / MARCH 2, 1977

By July 1, 1978:

1. I will be an outstanding Los Angeles City Fire
Department employee.

2. I will have a Master's degree.

3. I will be producing carved-wood and leaded-
glass objects for income.

By July 1, 1980:

1. I will no longer depend on the LAFD as a prime
source of income.

2. I will have a Doctorate degree.

3. I will have paid for and established an income-
producing carved-wood and leaded-glass business.

By July 1, 1982:

1. I will retire from the Los Angeles City Fire Department.

2. I will be a successful teacher of psychology and
philosophy.

3. I will be the owner and manager of a successful
carved-wood and leaded-glass business.

I will accomplish these objectives as a result of
giving the most enthusiastic and efficient service of
which I am capable, rendering the fullest possible

quantity and the best possible quality of service in the capacity of employee, student, and business man.

This is an irrevocable contract I make with myself.

Robert R. Porter

Here is a magnificent career goal. Bob achieved his goal for 1978 and now has his Master's. It will be interesting to watch his career.

GOAL CONTRACT / DECEMBER 31, 1973

Forthwith and for the foreseeable future my goals are:

To increase my self-confidence and develop a more positive approach to life in general, so that, as each new school year approaches I will be so sure of myself and my own ability that the first day of term with the new class will be very successful.

To support and assist my husband in every way possible in achieving his career and personal goals.

To become a more effective and loving mother by utilizing a more positive and dynamic approach with my children.

I will have achieved this as a result of giving the most efficient service of which I am capable, rendering the fullest possible quantity and the best possible quality of service in the capacity of wife, mother, and teacher.

This is an irrevocable contract that I make with myself.

Barbara Hamilton

Barbara is the teacher I wrote about in Chapter 6. Notice her goal relative to the new school year.

8 RASCON I

Now we come to RASCON and the psychophysical method of using systematic relaxation to get control of your biocomputer. This is the last and most demanding part of the cybernetic principles we have been discussing in this book.

I suppose if I were a snake-oil salesman or didn't really believe in what I am saying, this would be the ideal time to assure you that there's absolutely nothing to learning RASCON. One best-selling self-help author pretends to tell his readers all they need to know about two different relaxation techniques in just 61 words! (Reminds me of those ads that assure the gullible that by using a miraculous new system they can learn to play the piano like Horowitz in a month simply by practicing 15 minutes a day.)

Learning RASCON isn't that easy. To be more

precise, although learning RASCON isn't hard in itself, it will require some effort on your part, and you will have to follow the step-by-step procedures with care.

Perhaps the most tedious part is memorizing the key words and word formulas. There is only one shortcut you can take, and that is to make a tape recording so that you can play it back to yourself repeatedly during your leisure time.

If you have a cassette player, I suggest you use a C60 cassette and record the six- to seven-minute systematic relaxation, together with the entire "thought formula." If you wish, you can write to Psychofeedback Seminars, P.O. Box 49454, Los Angeles, California 90049, about the availability of a cassette.

The exercises which I will be asking you to do, after using RASCON a specific number of times, may seem strange to you. But they nevertheless have an important purpose: to train the subjective imagination. We all came into the world with the ability to use our imagination subjectively, but the majority of people lose this ability, and, as the split-brain research has shown, attempt to lead successful lives using only half their brains. The exercises giving your right hemisphere some work are for the purpose of training your imagination, thereby retrieving the ability of using both brain hemispheres in the most effective possible way.

Please do not do these exercises out of sequence or try to do them before you have used RASCON the required number of times. If you try to do them too soon, you will be unable to do them. They are designed to fulfill a second function, i.e., indicate to yourself the degree of proficiency you have achieved in gaining control over your biocomputer. I will give you the exact way to do these exercises as we come to them, and I shall tell you when you should do them.

From this moment forward, I want you to start being aware *at all times* of your own thoughts, the Input into your biocomputer. I want you to start cutting out the little negatives which can creep into your conversation without your even being aware that they have become a habit. For good or ill, the most important habits we have are our habits of thought.

Start with the response you habitually give to a question that is asked of you many times during the course of the day: "Hi, how are you?" Don't, by the gods, please DO NOT say, "Not bad," or "Could be better," or "I've been worse," "Heck, this is Monday, ask me tomorrow," or any of the other damned silly, facetious, and pitiful things said by people who aren't paying attention to the cybernetic implications of their words. Not even in jest—in fun—should you use these expressions.

Start using big expressive words: *terrific, fantastic, marvelous, magnificent, outstanding, wonderful, stupendous*. I have a list of about ten words which I use. You may find this habit a little difficult to develop. The reason for this is that you will be too concerned about what the other person is thinking, but *that* is the last thing you should be concerned about! What he is thinking is his Input and, in the short term, there is not a thing you can do about that! To be sure, as you adopt this *habit,* you will get some funny looks. Actually, until your friends and associates get used to your giving this kind of response, it can be amusing to watch their reactions.

"Hi, Joe, how are you?"

"Fantastic!"

There is instant disbelief in his quick "Are you?" Then he looks more intently at you, and you just know he is thinking, "I wonder what's going on here." The word I really enjoy using is "INVINCIBLE"—that one nearly knocks them over!

You may say, "How can I say I feel fantastic if I feel the opposite? I've got to be honest with myself." Wrong! This is the excuse people trot out for not controlling the Input into their biocomputers. The one thing over which you have absolute control is your own thoughts. It is *this* that puts you in a position to control your own destiny. You know that 99 percent of what you do every day is done as a matter of habit—Output from your bio-computer which is as good, or bad, as the Input.

It was for *this purpose,* and this purpose *only,* that you were given a willpower—the third function of the RAS. I might add that if you fail to control your own thoughts you will have difficulty in controlling anything else. If you want to be honest about something, be honest about that.

Let me illustrate exactly what I mean by telling you of something that happened while I was courting my wife, Adita.

Adita lost her first husband in March 1969. For her, the death of her husband, whom she loved dearly, was not merely a tragedy, it was an emotional catastrophe. She was so stricken with grief that by September she decided that she had to get away from California because she was too close to everything with which her husband had been associated. She decided to go to Europe and live there for one year.

We met socially on December 26, 1969, in Athens, where I was doing some business. I had always been a bachelor, and I found myself powerfully attracted to this lovely woman. Adita is a sister of the late movie star, Maria Montez, but she is much more beautiful. Our mutual attraction quickly developed into something serious and we soon became inseparable.

Yet Adita could not come to terms with the memory of her husband. Every day, and sometimes two, even three times in a day, she would cry bitter, pitiful tears of sorrow.

One day, about six weeks after we had met, I went into her suite in the hotel. She was standing by the window, looking at nothing, with tears streaming down her face. I stepped across the room, took her arm, sat her down, and said, "Listen, my darling, you *must* stop this. He has gone, and no amount of crying is going to bring him back."

Still crying, she said, "I can't. I can't help thinking of all the pain and suffering he went through."

"No, no, no, you do not have to do that. From now on, I want you to do something for me. Every time you feel the sting of tears behind your eyes, I want you to *immediately* change your thoughts. I want you to *immediately* think of some happy, joyous time you spent with him. Then you will find the sting will disappear and a little smile will come to the corners of your mouth."

Within about four or five weeks, all the crying had stopped.

Look again at what she had said: *"I can't help thinking . . ."* But that was the one thing she did not have to do! While she willfully allowed sorrowful thoughts into her biocomputer, her Output was sorrowful. When using her willpower *she chose* to think sunny, happy thoughts, her Output became sunny and happy.

I do not want you to misunderstand me. Of course her sorrow and grief were the most natural thing, and of course she had to shed tears. This is part of the mechanism of release. But at the same time, I would like you to keep in mind that this happened nearly one year after her loss.

When Coué said to his patients and followers, "You must deliberately and consciously say to yourself many times in the course of the day, 'Each and every day in every way I get better and better,'" what was he doing? By giving them this simple "thought formula," he was asking them to control the Input of information into their biocomputers and, as we know, the majority of them did get better and better.

"Each and every day in every way I get better and better" is a wonderful little phrase, not only because it is so easy to say, but also because it is all embracing. It does not say, in selling, in presentations, in closing, in administration, in golfing, in homemaking, in typing, or any one thing, does a person get better and better. It says "in every way." So, get in the habit of deliberately thinking this little thought.

What happens when a person deliberately thinks certain thoughts is well illustrated by the case of Mr. Spock. For five years actor Leonard Nimoy played Mr. Spock, chief officer on *Star Trek*. For five years *he had to* deliberately think specific thoughts because Mr. Spock is guided solely by logic. The result?

> *Spock had a big, big effect on me. I am so much more Spock-like today than when I first played the part in 1965 that you wouldn't recognize me. I'm not talking about appearance,* but thought processes. *Doing that character, I learned so much about* rational, logical thought *that it* reshaped my life.

And the same thing is going to happen with you.

I have stressed the importance of the Output (habit) of having a positive attitude early in this chapter because it is—or should be—so pervasive a quality that it almost falls outside the formal limits of RASCON.

To make this habit automatic and effortless, the following is the Input of information—the thought formula— which you should start to memorize.

> *Each and every morning when I wake up, I wake up with a very positive attitude. This positive attitude stays with me all day. I am aware of negative people and negative situations that I come into contact with at all times during the course of the day but they only cause me to be more positive. I am aware of any negative thought which happens*

to slip into my mind, but as I become aware of it,
which is immediately, I reject it as a spurious
thought.

There are two other formulas or Inputs that I want you to
memorize before you start to learn RASCON. The first
should be used at the end of the systematic relaxation
and before you Input the thought formula relative to
having a positive attitude, confidence, etc. The second
should be used when you terminate each session.

Here is the beginning formula:

Now I will use RASCON.
Each and every time I use RASCON I will be-
come more deeply relaxed and be able to use RAS-
CON faster than the time before.

This is the closing formula:

In a moment, I will stop using RASCON.
Physically, mentally, and emotionally, I feel
terrific, and I feel very energetic. On the count of
four, RASCON will stop. One, two, three, four.

These formulas alert the biocomputer that it is about to
receive—or stop receiving—a special kind of Input. It is a
little like the formulas "Start program" and "End program" used with a mechanical computer.

At this point I must get a little ahead of myself!
When you have completed the systematic relaxation and
have inserted the "Positive Attitude" Input, you should
spend two to three minutes using Psychofeedback—
inserting into your biocomputer the results of your past
performance—remembering some incidents in your life
when you felt particularly successful—some close you
made, if you are a salesman; some case you won, if you

are a lawyer; some honor you won, if you are a student; the day you got married; or even the highest bowling score you ever made.

I am assuming that you have already completed your goal contract so you should spend an additional two or three minutes inserting into your biocomputer the results of your present performance—imagining that you have already achieved your goal.

The key to achieving RASCON itself—to deactivating the RAS—lies in a psychophysiological technique which involves systematic relaxation. In time, you will be able to bypass this technique entirely and go straight to RASCON whenever you wish. But to begin with, you must practice. Every time you use RASCON, it has a cumulative effect, a kind of compounding, and the length of time required to go through systematic relaxation will gradually be decreased. After you have practiced for a while, you will be able to use RASCON with the ease with which you use a light switch.

But *you must not be impatient*. Although the *number of times* you use systematic relaxation is the key to shortening the time in which you achieve RASCON, do not try to hurry the process too much. When I teach a class, it takes eight weeks. You should allow at least a six-week period for practice sessions.

Systematic relaxation is accomplished through a monologue you will conduct with yourself. As you memorize the monologue, notice that for each section of your anatomy the words are more or less the same, which makes it easy. Read the words out loud ten or twenty times so you get the feel of them on your tongue. Then when you use them, they will not seem strange to you. You should not hurry the words. Walter Cronkite, reading the news, speaks at a conversational speed which is just a little too fast. The monologue should take not less than 6 minutes or more than 7.

On the following pages are the words you must at

first use to effect the systematic physical relaxation leading to RASCON. Then, on subsequent pages, you will see
that the monologue gets shorter.

Learn to use the various monologues in four stages.
The 6- to 7-minute monologue should be used 14 times;*
the 4- to 5-minute monologue, 14 times; the 2- to 3-minute
monologue, 14 times; and the 1- to 2-minute monologue,
14 times, for a total of 56 times. After this, all you will
have to do to use RASCON is say to yourself, silently and
meaningfully: "Four, my legs are relaxed. Three, my
torso is relaxed. Two, my shoulders and arms are relaxed.
One, my entire body is relaxed." Eventually, after, say,
two or three years, you will be able to use it without any
words at all.

Say the words quietly to yourself. If you try to
think the monologue through, you will have difficulty in
concentrating and excluding other thoughts.

You will see that if you use the monologues once a
day, the four steps will each take two weeks, for a total of
eight weeks. Assuming you stick to an eight-week, once-a-
day program, the first thing you should do is make a plan
as to when and where. Regarding the former, let me first
tell you the time you should *not* do this is in bed at night.
If you do it there, you will simply go to sleep. In fact, you
should not even try to do it late at night because the same
thing will happen.

The best time is first thing in the morning, before
the onset of the day's activities. But whatever time you
pick, set the same time each day. Otherwise, you may
procrastinate and push the time back repeatedly until
you fall into the trap of trying to do a double stint the
following day.

As to where, pick anywhere that you can be sure
you will not be disturbed for fifteen minutes—at least, for

---

*Actually, I shall ask you to use these monologues a few
more times in connection with some special exercises.

about the first thirty times that you practice. Be strict with yourself about this: Take the phone off the hook and lock the door. There are no special rules for the position. Adita always lies down on a divan in her dressing room for her daily use of RASCON; she dislikes the upright position I prefer. I, on the other hand, dislike lying down, so I sit in my chair in the studio.

A question frequently asked by my students is; "Is there a sensation with RASCON?" There is no sensation, so do not look for one. There is, however, what I might call a state of "ultraconsciousness." "Altered state of consciousness" is one of these esoteric terms I mentioned in the Introduction which can cause a great deal of confusion if it is to be conceptualized. Ultraconsciousness, on the other hand, is very clear as a concept because people are literally more conscious when they use RASCON. All their senses are sharpened. When they hear sounds, they are slightly louder.

I will ask you to do two things before beginning the systematic relaxation. The first is to take a deep breath and then continue to breathe just a little deeper than you usually do. Just a little, not exaggeratedly so. The second thing is to close your eyes. It is quite impossible for you to concentrate on the dialogue that I want you to use with your eyes open. If your eyes are open, inevitably all the information you will be processing through them will distract you.

Start the monologue as follows:

I'm thinking of my feet and I'm allowing my feet to relax. I'm thinking of my feet and I'm allowing my feet to relax. As I think of my feet, I can feel my feet becoming more relaxed. I'll wiggle my toes a little to become more aware of my feet, and as I do so, I can feel my feet becoming more relaxed. My feet now are completely and utterly relaxed. Relaxation continues over my insteps past my ankles to the calves of my legs.

I'm thinking of my calves and I'm allowing my calves to relax. I'm thinking of my calves and I'm allowing my calves to relax. As I think of my calves, I can feel my calves become more relaxed. I'll twitch the muscles in my calves to become more aware of them, and as I twitch the muscles in my calves, I can feel my calves becoming more relaxed. My calves now are completely and utterly relaxed.

Relaxation continues up over my knees to my thighs.

I'm thinking of my thighs and I'm allowing my thighs to relax. I'm thinking of my thighs and I'm allowing my thighs to relax. As I think of my thighs, I can feel my thighs becoming more relaxed. My thighs now are completely and utterly relaxed. I have allowed both of my legs to become so relaxed that my legs are now feeling very limp. I have allowed both of my legs to become so relaxed that my legs are now feeling very limp, and they are beginning to feel just a little heavy. Relaxation is like a blanket being pulled up over my hips and now covers my abdomen. I'm allowing all the muscles around my stomach to relax. I'm allowing all the muscles around my stomach to become relaxed. As I allow all the muscles around my stomach to become completely and utterly relaxed, my stomach feels very limp. Now I will allow all the muscles around my rib cage and my midriff and diaphragm to relax.

As I allow the muscles around my rib cage and midriff and diaphragm to become completely and utterly relaxed, I realize that I'm breathing more deeply.

I'm breathing deeply and rhythmically, and with each rhythmic breath I take, I'm becoming more and more pleasantly relaxed. Relaxation spreads around to my back, my back form fits the chair with comfort and ease. I'm sitting (or lying) very comfortably and very contentedly. I'm sitting very comfortably and very contentedly. As I allow all the muscles in my back to relax it seems as though I'm blending with the chair on which I'm sitting [or the bed which I'm lying upon].

Relaxation continues up my spine through my central nervous system, relaxing muscle and tissue and sinew all over my body; and as it continues up my back, under my shoulder blades, over my shoulder blades, I can feel my shoulders relaxing. I'm allowing my shoulders to relax. I'm allowing my shoulders to relax.

As I allow my shoulders to become more relaxed, I can feel my shoulders begin to droop.

As I allow my shoulders to become more relaxed I can feel my shoulders drooping and sagging as they become completely and utterly relaxed. My arms are hanging from my shoulders in a very loose, limp manner. My arms are hanging from my shoulders in a very loose, limp manner, and I'm allowing my arms to relax. I'm allowing my arms to relax. Relaxation is spreading from my upper arms to my forearms and to my hands.

Relaxation is spreading from my upper arms to my forearms and to my hands. I have allowed both of my arms to become so relaxed that my arms are now feeling very limp.

I have allowed both of my arms to become so relaxed that my arms are now feeling very limp, and they also are beginning to feel just a little heavy.

Now I'll allow all the muscles around my neck and my throat to relax. I'm allowing all the muscles around my neck and my throat to become completely and utterly relaxed.

As I allow all the muscles around my neck and my throat to relax, my head begins to feel rather heavy and droops toward my chest. [If you are upright, really allow these muscles to relax and your head to droop forward. You cannot possibly be relaxed if you keep your neck stiff and upright.]

Now I'll allow all of my facial muscles to relax. I'm allowing all of my facial muscles to relax.

I'll erase all the frown lines from my forehead and between my eyebrows. I'll erase all the frown lines from my forehead and between my eyebrows. As I allow all of my facial muscles to relax, my face seems to be bathed in a gentle feeling of relaxation.

I've allowed the smallest muscles in my body— the muscles around my eyelids—to relax and my eyelids feel very heavy. I've allowed the smallest muscles in my body—the muscles around my eyelids—to become so relaxed that my eyelids are feeling very heavy. And I slip gently into a deep state of complete and utter relaxation. I'm going deeper and deeper into this wonderful relaxation. I'm breathing deeply and rhythmically, and with each rhythmic breath I take, I become more and more pleasantly relaxed. All the sounds I can hear in the background are only helping me to become more relaxed and go deeper into this complete and utter relaxation.

Now I will use RASCON. Each and every time I use RASCON, I will become more deeply relaxed and be able to use RASCON faster than the time before. [Repeat this last sentence with slightly more emphasis.]

Each and every morning when I wake up, I wake up with a very positive attitude. This positive attitude stays with me all day. I am aware of negative people and negative situations that I come into contact with at all times during the course of the day, but they only cause me to be more positive. I am aware of any negative thought which happens to slip into my mind, but as I become aware of it—which is immediately—I reject it as spurious.

[Spend 2 or 3 minutes using Psychofeedback, remembering some occasion in your past when you felt eminently successful.]

In a moment I will stop using RASCON. I feel wonderful in every way. Physically, mentally, and emotionally, I feel terrific, and I feel very energetic. On the count of four, RASCON will stop. One [pause]. Two [pause]. Three [pause]. Four.

Before moving ahead, let me make two brief comments about what you have just read. First; although memorizing the relaxation part of the monologue may seem tiresome to you now, it's really much easier than it looks. It follows a simple, logical progression, and it is filled with conventional repetitions. Also, you can simply put them on tape, thus eliminating entirely the need for memorization.

Second; although the systematic relaxation instructions are the technique of the hypnotist, that is where the similarity ends. Using RASCON you are not only fully conscious, but fully—even extraordinarily—in control of yourself at all times.

Now let us return to our practice sessions. When you have completed your first group of 6- to 7-minute sessions, there is an exercise you should do to verify the degree of control you have achieved over your biocomputer. You should do this exercise *only* after you have used RASCON, a minimum of fourteen times. Do it at least three times to satisfy yourself that you have achieved this degree of control. By that I mean three separate additional 6- to 7-minute systematic relaxation sessions which can be done consecutively in a matter of 25 minutes.

This exercise, which I call the swallowing exercise, illustrates the first small step you will take in the control of your biocomputer. To understand the purpose of the exercise, bear in mind the way the mechanism of swallowing and salivating ordinarily works.

Swallowing and salivating are entirely involuntary actions. You never have to *think consciously* of when and how you are to swallow because that is all taken care of by your biocomputer. If you are out in your garden and you catch the delicious aroma of someone barbecuing next door, what happens? Your nose picks up the smell, passes the information through to your biocomputer. (Remember, there is a neuron chain for everything you sense—see, *smell,* taste, hear, touch). As the information comes in, the biocomputer scans the Permanent Storage relative to smell and having found it, says, "Burning beef . . . ah, delicious cooking beef." And your mouth begins to water. Do you consciously have to think "mouth start watering"? Of course you do not.

However, when you do the swallowing exercise in the way I want you to do it, something different is going to happen. The exercise is to imagine that you are feeling thirsty, that there is only one way you can quench your thirst—by swallowing—but that you will only swallow on a particular count. Here is the monologue which you must use after you have completed the preliminaries of systematic relaxation:

> *I'm feeling very thirsty. I'm going to count from one to five. As I count from one to five, I will become progressively more thirsty. There is only one way I can quench my thirst, and that is by swallowing. I will feel an uncontrollable urge to swallow to quench my thirst exactly on the count of five, and not before. One. I'm feeling very thirsty and my throat is very dry. Two. My throat is becoming more dry and I feel even more thirsty. Three. The saliva in my mouth is becoming slightly watery in anticipation of my swallowing, and*

> *my thirst is increasing. Four. Now I'm parched
> with thirst. I'm desperately thirsty. Five.*

If you have done the things I have asked you to do, you
will swallow immediately after you say the word "Five."

You will say to yourself, "Well, yes, of course, I
made myself swallow." And that will be correct; you did
make yourself swallow. *But not from the conscious level.*
You gave your biocomputer a command and it carried it
out.

If you have difficulty in believing this, then do it
again, but this time *change the count.* Go through exactly
the same procedure, changing the monologue only by
saying, "I'm going to count from one to *six".* When you
get to "Five", try to swallow. You will find that you
cannot do so. Something stops you. It is your biocomputer, to which you have now given a different command.

You have just demonstrated your ability to control
what would normally be an involuntary reaction. Like
those people who have become adept with electronic biofeedback machines, you have shown that you have begun
to master the technique of making your automatic nervous system do what you want it to do. This mastery will
increase dramatically with practice.

You have now completed the first phase of the
practice sessions. In this phase you learned the basic
systematic relaxation techniques and how to turn RAS-
CON on and off. You also inserted one thought formula
into your biocomputer: the "positive attitude" thought
formula.

In the following phases, you will reduce both the
time you spend on systematic relaxation and add to the
number of thought formulas you are inserting. In the
next phase, a new thought formula we shall add deals
with self-confidence.

There are essentially two sets of circumstances in
which people experience lack of self-confidence. When a

person is called upon to do things he has done infrequently, if ever—including meeting people he is not accustomed to meeting; and when he has had an experience which has not produced the desired results.

What are the reasons for a lack of confidence under these circumstances? Only two: a lack of understanding of Psychofeedback and Coué's Law. And unfortunately, even *with* full understanding, a person can still sometimes experience a lack of confidence in an unguarded moment. The person who says that he has never experienced a lack of confidence in his lifetime is as full of false bravado as the salesperson who says that he has never experienced call reluctance.

The biocomputer is a very selfish mechanism. As it takes you through life, guiding and directing your every movement and action, accomplishing the innumerable goals of minor and major importance, it is concerned with one thing only: your safety and your happiness, steering you away from whatever you consider to be unpleasant and toward whatever you consider to be pleasant. But it must always act upon the information which *you insert into it.*

Look back over your life. Have there been occasions when you experienced a lack of confidence? Is there a particular type of person who causes you to feel uncomfortable and unsure of yourself? Do not say "never," because you will not be telling the truth.

In each of the next fourteen practice sessions with RASCON, we will spend about two minutes putting some *new information* about self-confidence in your biocomputer. In your imagination, see yourself handling those threatening situations and difficult people with poise and supreme confidence. Remember: the biocomputer, cannot tell the difference between a real and an imagined experience. The old information is still and always will be in storage, but the more times you use your imagination in the way I have asked you to use it, the more permanently stored becomes the new information, and the less effect the old storage will have upon your future actions.

As to the future, we want your biocomputer to respond to the following Input, which you must memorize.

At this moment I feel supremely confident in my own ability and accordingly I act and behave in a very confident manner. I have complete confidence in my ability to handle and control any and every situation with which I am confronted in a way that is best suited for me to achieve my goals.

In case your confidence in yourself is minimal, it may be necessary for you to spend longer than two minutes—say five minutes, and for more than just the next fourteen times. Only you know and can decide what is best for you, now that you understand the mechanism. Certainly, if you have very little self confidence you should not expect an instant transformation. It does not happen that way and yet happen it *must*. On the other hand you may already have supreme confidence in yourself and your ability in which case there may be a tendency on your part to think that you do not need to memorize the Input relative to confidence. I hope you do not.

The same remarks apply to another thought formula we shall insert during this phase: a formula having to do with energy. You may be a very energetic person, and may think that you do not need the Input to produce more energy, but I hope you will reconsider. We all have much more potential energy than any of us ever uses. The purpose of our energy-related thought formula is to convert more of that potential energy into actual, usable energy:

I now have more energy than I've ever had in my entire life. I know that I have the mental and

*physical resources to do twice as much as I have
been doing, so I demand that I have an abundance
of tireless energy with which to pursue and achieve
my goals. I do not waste my energy on unnecessary
and bad emotions which I know are bad for me and
which I recognize are bad for me.*

The last sentence in this Input requires some explanation,
and you may wish to expand upon it slightly. There are
two major ways in which people waste an enormous
amount of energy.

The first is on worry. Our lives are made up of a
never-ending series of decisions, from the trivial minute-
by-minute decisions to the matters of life or death.

All these decisions, regardless of their degree of
importance, are attendant upon a set of *facts*. People who
are securely in control of their own affairs know this, and
when called upon to make a decision, they evaluate the
facts carefully before deciding. But, interestingly, they
make their evaluations rapidly. It is surprising how
many people go over and over the facts, unnecessarily
wasting their energy. It is even more surprising—and
there is nothing mitigating about this—that so many
people worry about a decision they have *already made*.
That truly is an exercise in futility.

Another way that people waste an enormous
amount of energy is in disliking people. What ghastly
Input are expressions and thoughts such as; "I can't
stand him," "She irritates the life out of me," "I think
he's an absolute pain." Even as I wrote the words,
thereby allowing the thought to enter my mind, I felt a
shiver go up my spine. What an abysmal and pathetic
waste of energy.

I do not want you to think that I consider myself a
paragon of virtue, because I am not. However, I do practice what I teach and I can emphatically tell you that
there is not a person I know whom I dislike. I am cer-

tainly not like Will Rogers who is reputed to have said, "Never did meet the man I didn't like," because it is impossible to like everyone with whom you come into contact. But I can tell you, with just as much emphasis, that if I am forced into the company of a person who has characteristics I find objectionable, then, by the gods, I am not going to waste my energy disliking him or her. I ignore them.

This habit, which in essence means controlling your emotions, is not an easy one to develop, but develop it you must. We have an abundance of energy but not so much that we can afford to squander it on petty dislikes. Your reaction, if you have this bad habit, may be "there's nothing petty about the way I dislike so and so." Isn't there? What is the criterion by which you have arrived at this conclusion? However you answer, the criterion should be, "Is so-and-so doing me any harm or affecting my work?" If he is, do something about the situation. If not, be civil and ignore him. Mentally.

Paradoxically, one of the major aspects of being energetic is being relaxed. People who are hypertense almost never use their energy output to any good purpose and can make themselves sick as well. Being physically relaxed does not mean being mentally relaxed, but the reverse. You will find that as your biocomputer responds to the Input below, you will become much more alert and mentally productive, and you will observe a considerable increase in your problem solving capacity.

> When I stop using RASCON, the physical me—my body—remains in a relaxed state. Each and every day, for the entire day, I am physically relaxed although my mind is always exceptionally alert and productive.

Now let us run through a practice session. You now are ready to shorten the systematic relaxation to 4- to 5-

minutes as follows, always remembering to first close
your eyes, taking a deep breath and continuing to breathe
a little deeper than you usually do.

> *I'm thinking of my feet and I'm allowing my feet to
> relax. As I think of my feet, I can feel my feet
> becoming more relaxed. My feet now are com-
> pletely and utterly relaxed. Relaxation continues
> over my insteps past my ankles to the calves of my
> legs.*
>
> *I'm thinking of my calves and I'm allowing my
> calves to relax. As I think of my calves, I can feel
> my calves become more relaxed. My calves now are
> completely and utterly relaxed.*
>
> *Relaxation continues up over my knees to my
> thighs.*
>
> *I'm thinking of my thighs and I'm allowing my
> thighs to relax. As I think of my thighs, I can feel
> my thighs becoming more relaxed. My thighs now
> are completely and utterly relaxed.*
>
> *I have allowed both of my legs to become so
> relaxed that my legs are now feeling very limp. I
> have allowed both of my legs to become so relaxed
> that my legs are now feeling very limp, and they
> are beginning to feel just a little heavy.*
>
> *Relaxation is like a blanket being pulled up over
> my hips and now covers my abdomen. I'm allowing
> all the muscles around my stomach to relax. As I
> allow all the muscles around my stomach to be-
> come completely and utterly relaxed, my stomach
> feels very limp. Now I will allow all the muscles
> around my rib cage and my midriff and diaphragm
> to relax.*
>
> *As I allow all the muscles around my rib cage
> and midriff and diaphragm to become completely
> and utterly relaxed, I realize that I'm breathing
> more deeply.*

I'm breathing deeply and rhythmically, and with each rhythmic breath I take, I'm becoming more and more pleasantly relaxed. Relaxation spreads around to my back. I'm sitting (or lying) very comfortably and very contentedly. As I allow all the muscles in my back to relax, it seems as though I'm blending with the chair which I'm sitting on [or the bed which I'm lying upon].

Relaxation continues up my spine through my central nervous system, relaxing muscle and tissue and sinew all over my body, and, as it continues up my back, under my shoulder blades, over my shoulder blades, I can feel my shoulders relaxing. I'm allowing my shoulders to relax.

As I allow my shoulders to become more relaxed, I can feel my shoulders begin to droop. As I allow my shoulders to become more relaxed, I can feel my shoulders drooping and sagging as they become completely and utterly relaxed.

My arms are hanging from my shoulders in a very loose, limp manner. I'm allowing my arms to relax. Relaxation is spreading from my upper arms to my forearms and to my hands.

Relaxation is spreading from my upper arms to my forearms and to my hands. I have allowed both of my arms to become so relaxed that my arms are now feeling very limp.

I have allowed both of my arms to become so relaxed that my arms are now feeling very limp, and they also are beginning to feel just a little heavy.

I'm allowing all the muscles around my neck and my throat to become completely and utterly relaxed.

As I allow all the muscles around my neck and my throat to relax, my head begins to feel rather heavy and droops toward my chest. [Do not forget,

*if you are using the upright position, really allow
these muscles to relax and your head to droop
forward.]*

*Now I'll allow all of my facial muscles to relax.
I'm allowing all of my facial muscles to relax.*

*I'll erase all the frown lines from my forehead
and between my eyebrows. As I allow all of my
facial muscles to relax, my face seems to be bathed
in a gentle feeling of relaxation.*

*I've allowed the smallest muscles in my body—
the muscles around my eyelids—to relax, and my
eyelids feel very heavy. I've allowed the smallest
muscles in my body—the muscles around my
eyelids—to become so relaxed that my eyelids are
feeling very heavy. And I slip gently into a deep
state of complete and utter relaxation. I'm going
deeper and deeper into this wonderful relaxation.
I'm breathing deeply and rhythmically, and with
each rhythmic breath I take, I become more and
more pleasantly relaxed. All the sounds I can hear
in the background are only helping me to become
more relaxed and go deeper into this complete and
utter relaxation.*

*Each and every time I use RASCON, I will be-
come more deeply relaxed and be able to use RAS-
CON faster than the time before. Each and every
time I use RASCON, I will become more deeply
relaxed and be able to use RASCON faster than the
time before.*

*Each and every morning when I wake up, I wake
up with a very positive attitude. This positive attitude stays with me all day. I am aware of negative
people and negative situations that I come into
contact with at all times during the course of the
day, but they only cause me to be more positive. I
am aware of any negative thought which happens
to slip into my mind, but as I become aware of it,*

*which is immediately, I reject it as a spurious
thought.*

*At this moment, I feel supremely confident in my
own ability, and accordingly I act and behave in a
very confident manner. I have complete confidence
in my ability to handle and control any and every
situation with which I am confronted in a way that
is best suited for me to achieve my goals.*

*I now have more energy than I've ever had in my
entire life. I know that I have the mental and
physical resources to do twice as much as I have
been doing so I demand that I have an abundance
of tireless energy with which to pursue and achieve
my goals. I do not waste my energy on unnecessary
and bad emotions which I know are bad for me and
which I recognize are bad for me.*

*When I stop using RASCON, the physical me—
my body—remains in a relaxed state. Each and
every day, for the entire day, I am physically relaxed although my mind is always exceptionally
alert and productive.*

Spend 2 or 3 minutes using Psychofeedback, remembering some occasion in your past when you felt eminently
successful. Spend 2 or 3 minutes imagining yourself as an
even more confident person. Spend 2 or 3 minutes imagining you have already reached your goal.

*In a moment I will stop using RASCON. I feel
wonderful in every way. Physically, mentally, and
emotionally, I feel terrific and I feel very energetic.
On the count of four, RASCON will stop. One. Two.
Three. Four.*

After you have used RASCON an additional fourteen
times, which will bring the total up to a minimum of
twenty-eight, plus the extras you did when you did the

swallowing exercise, you will be ready for the next exercise.

This hand exercise is the second step—but still only a small one—which you are taking in the control you are achieving over your biocomputer. As with the first exercise, it is necessary that you do this only three times.

After taking 4 to 5 minutes on the systematic relaxation, I want you to raise your right forearm and bend your arm at the elbow, keeping your hand about 12 inches away from your body. Keep the back of your hand toward you, and spread your fingers and thumb as far apart as possible. Then I want you to imagine—as vividly as possible—that a strong elastic band has been put around your four fingers. The elastic band is black, 2 inches in diameter, half an inch deep, and a quarter of an inch thick.

As you imagine this and concentrate your attention on your hand, say to yourself: "The elastic band is getting tighter and tighter. I can feel it pulling my fingers together. I'm trying to strain against it, but it is just too strong for me. It keeps getting tighter and tighter around my fingers, pulling my fingers together, pulling them together, pulling them together."

Repeat this two or three times. When your fingers touch each other, tell yourself, "The elastic band has now broken and fallen from my fingers." Allow your hand to return to your lap and stop using RASCON.

This exercise is contrary to human physiology. It should not be possible to draw your fingers together merely by imagining that an elastic band is around them, and yet, if you have used RASCON twenty-eight times you should be able to do the exercise without any difficulty. You will notice that you are starting to use your imagination subjectively.

9 RASCON II

As I pointed out to you at the end of Chapter 3, for every good and productive habit, there is an opposite, bad, and unproductive habit.

One such habit is procrastination. It is a human characteristic to put off until *next week* what should have been done *last month*. This is one of those habits which we program into our biocomputer in our formative years without being aware.

There are some habits which dog a person of endeavor. They are often the Achilles heel of that person. They are like devils intent upon frustrating the most purposeful of individuals. These devils often go in pairs, hand in hand, hounding the traveller through life's journey. Procrastination has a brother devil whose name is indecision. Taking x as the measure of Output, if you have x amount of procrastination, it will inevitably be accompanied by x amount of indecision, and vice versa.

I cannot promise that when you use RASCON and Input the information relative to having a "do-it-now" attitude that all proscrastination will cease. That is too much to expect. However, I can promise you that as a result of this Input, you will have more of a "do-it-now" attitude related to your life and your work. This in turn will result in your becoming a more decisive person, because the corollary of the previous paragraph is that these two habits—angels, we might call them, if we use the same analogy—also go hand in hand, and by the same measure.

The Input for having more of a "do-it-now" attitude is:

> *I now have more of a do-it-now attitude related to my life and my work than ever before. That which needs to be done today, I do today, because I want to and because the achievement of my goal[s] and my happiness are the most important things in my life.*

Everybody has problems. But what is a "problem"? A problem can either be composed of a set of known facts to which there is no immediate resolution, or it can be composed of a mixture of known and unknown facts. The second is the more usual kind of problem, and it can be solved only by making an estimate based on probabilities. If you can learn to make accurate estimates based on probabilities, you will have what is called "good judgment." But you will never learn this valuable skill unless you try, and unless you are willing to make decisions.

This is why I want you to make a three-pronged attack on the bad habit of indecision. Your biocomputer must respond to the Input of information relative to not wasting energy on dysfunctional worry. It must respond to the Input of information relative to you having more of a "do-it-now" Output. The third prong of the attack is contained in this Input of information:

> *I am now a very decisive person. Whenever I'm faced with a problem, I quickly but carefully weigh up all the facts that are available to me regarding the problem; and on the basis of the facts, I make a decision. When the facts of the problem are not clearly known to me, I exercise sound judgment and base my decision on the most likely probabilities. When my decision calls for a course of action, I act upon my decision immediately, sure in the knowledge that I am in control of my own affairs and my own destiny.*

Now I would like to mention another important habit to cultivate: diligence.

When I write about diligence, I feel somewhat diffident because I know that it is impossible to write anything that does not sound hackneyed. There can be little doubt that any difficulty we have with this habit, which influences the attitude we adopt to our work, is largely due to the programming that went on in our childhood, when we were *made* to go to school. I do not suppose there is more than one child in a hundred who really enjoys being made to go to school. Unfortunately, this preference for having a good time at the expense of buckling down to school—and later real—work, deeply embedded in our Permanent Storage, carries over into our adult life.

There is a real possibility that you may be one of the people discovered by a 1973 survey of 25,000 families conducted by the Department of HEW. This survey reported that 80 percent of the breadwinners in the families said that they hated—notice that word—*hated* their work.

I sincerely hope that you are among the contented minority, but if you do happen to be one of the 80 percent, start immediately to be aware of such Input as "I hate my job," "I loathe my work," etc., because your biocomputer will respond accordingly. It will cause you to feel frustrated, and by inducing that feeling, it will indicate to you that it does not want you to work. I have already explained to you that the biocomputer integrates information in three ways: Word, Experiential, and Conceptual, But it processes all information concept by concept. There is Conceptual Storage for "hate," and there is other Conceptual Storage for "work." Surely you can see the necessity of keeping the two storage items as far apart as possible. Much better to Input information such as, "I don't enjoy the work I am doing currently, but I am working to change this situation," or something similar.

The Input for increasing the Output of diligence is:

> *In order to more quickly reach my goals, I work hard every day, and no day is too long for me. I plan my time effectively, and I work according to my plan. There is no slackening in my effort to reach my goal[s], and I look forward with pleasure to and I enjoy the hard work which is required of me that I may reach my goal[s].*

It does not matter what your work is, you will find that when this information becomes part of your Permanent Storage you will be doing more, working harder. It will not *seem* to you as though you are being more diligent. But the results will prove it.

The next part of the "thought formula" that I want you to start establishing as Permanent Storage relates to another habit which I consider to be one of the most important characteristics any human being can possess: resilience.

Resilience is the ability to not merely roll with the

punches, but to take one in the guts, go down to the canvas, shake your head, get up, and continue the fight. In case you think I am talking about courage, which I am not, I had better mix my metaphors and say that to be resilient is to be like a reed which bends in the wind and never breaks.

If I were a genie with the power of magic and could give my students anything they desired, I would give them an abundance of resilience. With that they could conquer the world. The resilient person does not admit the Word Storage "defeat" into his biocomputer. He regards defeat as a setback, but only a temporary one at that. Furthermore, he even regards temporary setbacks as the stepping-stones across the stream of life.

Sometimes you will experience temporary setbacks. If you do not, you are not striving towards a goal. When you do experience these setbacks, you will be better prepared to deal with them by having the correct Permanent Storage in your biocomputer.

The habitual Output of resilience is inextricably entwined with another habit, the Output of persistence. I don't think I need to say much about this habit, because I am confident that you already have the necessary Conceptual Storage in your biocomputer relative to the word "persistence." If you did not, nothing I could write would make much difference to you.

The Input of information for increasing both resilience and persistence is:

> *I realize that although I work hard and I am persistent in my effort to reach my goal(s), there are some things which I cannot control. In particular, I cannot control other people. In the event that people cause a temporary setback in my progress toward my goal[s], I recognize it for what it is; only a temporary setback. I am like a reed which bends in the wind and never breaks, and my persistence and*

> *tenacity in reaching my goal[s] is doubly strength-*
> *ened as a result of any temporary setback I may*
> *experience.*

If there is one item of Word Storage that triggers Conceptual Storage, it is "self-discipline."

When most people think of self-discipline, i.e., insert the Word Storage "self-discipline" into their biocomputer, the biocomputer responds with the Word/Con-
ceptual Storage of "effort" and "willpower." I have said
to you previously that the strengthening of the program
in your biocomputer must be done without invoking the
faculty of willpower. At least not in the way willpower is
thought of traditionally. This holds true for developing
the habit of "self-discipline," however much using "willpower" might seem necessary to achieve this goal.

You are *already* self-disciplined because you have
the intellectual capacity to know that society demands
this of you. It is with the same intellectual ability that
you must monitor the Output from your biocomputer. If
you have unproductive habits and habit patterns, only
you know about them, and only you can do anything
about them. What matters do you avoid dealing with? Do
not say that you never procrastinate because that will not
be the truth. Isolate these troublesome matters, then use
RASCON. *In your imagination,* see yourself dealing with
these matters with alacrity and dispatch. Are there situations which cause you to be indecisive? In your imagination, see yourself swiftly making the right decision. Are
you as diligent in your work as you should be? Do not say
that you are never lazy—it will not be the truth. Laziness
is one of the pleasures of self-indulgence. I enjoy being
lazy, but the program in my biocomputer will allow me to
indulge myself only at certain times and only for certain
periods, after which my Program sees to it that I dislike it
intensely. I certainly do not have to will myself to dislike
it—it happens automatically.

Are you habitually impatient with trying circumstances and people? Excessive impatience is an unproductive habit. When you use RASCON, imagine yourself dealing patiently with those trying circumstances and people.

All the foregoing are matters of self-discipline, and you must now input the following Word Storage:

> *From this moment, I discipline myself as I expect other people to be disciplined. I am very strict with myself with regard to all of my habits. I know that I am a conglomeration of habits and that it is only by establishing and maintaining good and productive habits that the achievement of my goals is assured. Therefore, I am at all times consciously aware of whatever bad habits I have and I constantly try to root them out and substitute them with good and productive habits.*

When you have used RASCON a minimum of twenty-eight times, you are ready to shorten the systematic relaxation to 2 to 3 minutes. You will notice that you do not start with the minor muscle assemblies of feet, calves, etc.; you start immediately with your legs, with the following monologue:

> *I am thinking of my legs and I am allowing my legs to relax. I am thinking of my legs and I am allowing my legs to relax. My legs are now completely and utterly relaxed. I have allowed both of my legs to become so relaxed that my legs are now feeling very limp.*
>
> *I have allowed both of my legs to become so relaxed that my legs are feeling very limp and heavy.*
>
> *Relaxation is like a blanket being pulled up over my hips and now covers the front of my body.*

I am allowing all the muscles in the front of my body to relax. I'm allowing all the muscles in the front of my body to relax. As I allow all the muscles in the front of my body to relax, I realize that I'm breathing more deeply.

I'm breathing deeply and rhythmically, and with each rhythmic breath I take, I'm becoming more and more pleasantly relaxed.

Relaxation spreads around to my back, and I'm allowing all the muscles in my back to relax.

Relaxation continues up my spine through my central nervous system, relaxing muscle and tissue and sinew all over my body. As it continues up my back over my shoulder blades, under my shoulder blades, I can feel my shoulders relaxing.

I'm allowing my shoulders to relax.

As I allow my shoulders to become more relaxed, I can feel my shoulders drooping and sagging.

My shoulders are drooping and sagging as they become completely and utterly relaxed.

My arms are hanging from my shoulders in a very loose, limp manner.

My arms are hanging from my shoulders in a very loose, limp manner, and as my arms become completely and utterly relaxed, my arms feel very limp and heavy.

As my arms become more relaxed, my arms feel very limp and heavy.

Now I'll allow all the muscles around my neck and my throat to relax, and my head feels rather heavy.

I'm allowing all of my facial muscles to relax.

I've allowed the smallest muscles in my body—the muscles around my eyelids—to relax, and my eyelids feel very heavy.

I've allowed the smallest muscles in my body—the muscles around my eyelids—to relax, and my eyelids feel very heavy.

And I slip gently into a deep state of complete and utter relaxation.

Input the information as per the previous chapter relative to positive attitude, confidence, energy, etc., and then continue with the new Input for "do it now," decisiveness, etc., as follows:

I now have more of a do it now attitude related to my life and my work than ever before. That which needs to be done today, I do today, because I want to and because the achievement of my goal[s] and my happiness are the most important things in my life.

I am now a very decisive person. Whenever I'm faced with a problem, I quickly but carefully weigh up all the facts that are available to me regarding the problem, and on the basis of the facts I make a decision. When the facts of the problem are not clearly known to me, I exercise sound judgment and base my decision on the most likely probabilities. When my decision calls for a course of action, I act upon my decision immediately, sure in the knowledge that I am in control of my own affairs and my own destiny.

I realize that although I work hard and I am persistent in my effort to reach my goal[s], there are some things which I cannot control. In particular I cannot control other people. In the event that people cause a temporary setback in my progress toward my goal[s], I recognize it for what it is; only a temporary setback. I am like a reed which bends in the wind and never breaks, and my persistence and tenacity in reaching my goal[s] is doubly strengthened as a result of any temporary setback I may experience.

From this moment I discipline myself as I expect other people to be disciplined. I am very strict with

> *myself with regard to all of my habits. I know that*
> *I am a conglomeration of habits, and that it is only*
> *by establishing and maintaining good and produc-*
> *tive habits that the achievement of my goals is*
> *assured. Therefore, I am at all times consciously*
> *aware of whatever bad habits I have, and I con-*
> *stantly try to root them out and substitute them*
> *with good and productive habits.*

Spend 2 to 5 minutes seeing yourself in your imagination as a much more successful person in *every way.* But concentrate particularly on that Output; those habits which we have discussed in this chapter.

Stop using RASCON in the usual way.

When you have used RASCON an additional fourteen times, which now brings the total up to a minimum of forty-two times, you will be ready to do the next exercise, which is a giant step forward in the control you are achieving over your biocomputer. I call this "the eye exercise," and I think it is going to surprise you.

You must imagine that your eyelids are glued together and that you cannot open them until you give your biocomputer a prearranged signal. Let me give you the words you will say to yourself and then I will discuss the exercise further.

Go through the systematic relaxation taking the required 2 to 3 minutes. (Incidentally, by this time you may be saying to yourself that you do not need to take that length of time to use RASCON. Please do not do that. Take the time that I ask you to take. It is important.) So, having deactivated your RAS, you then say to yourself as you imagine:

> *My eyelids are glued together.*
> *I am going to count from one to five. As I count*
> *from one to five, my eyelids will become progres-*
> *sively more tightly glued together. It will be impos-*

sible for me to open my eyes before I reach the count of five.

One. *My eyelids are glued together, stuck together, sealed together, and it is impossible for me to open my eyes.*

Two. *My eyelids are more tightly glued together, stuck together, bonded together, and it is impossible for me to open my eyes.*

Three. *It is as though the moisture around my eyes has turned to steel cement, and it is impossible for me to open my eyes.*

Four. *I will try to open my eyes, but the harder I try, the more tightly they become stuck together. [As you Input this information, really try to open your eyelids.]*

Five.

When you say "five" your eyelids will fly open. Allow them to close, and stop using RASCON in the usual way.

When you go through this sequence and get to "Four, I will try to open my eyes but the harder I try, etc.," it is important that you do not allow the thought to cross your mind—your RAS—that you will open your eyes. If you do, then of course your eyelids will fly open. But you know you can open your eyes and by not controlling the Input into your biocomputer, you will defeat the purpose of the exercise.

Of all your physical movements, at whatever level, the act of blinking your eyes is the most involuntary. Never do you have to think *when* and *how* to blink your eyes. It is entirely an unconditioned reflex. Blink your eyes a few times now, at this moment. Were you thinking consciously *how* to blink your eyes? When you can do this exercise, the act of blinking your eyes ceases to be an involuntary action; it becomes a controlled action. It is contrary to human physiology that simply by imagining that your eyelids are stuck together, they become so.

There is some Word Storage which can very easily be linked to the wrong Conceptual Storage. Such a word is *aggressiveness*. I would not want you to conceptualize this important word incorrectly by confusing it with a similar word of very different connotation: *aggression*.

Aggressive people are people who energetically attack the problems with which they are confronted. If the problems involve other individuals, as so often happens, an aggressive person first makes sure that the facts clearly call for a shift in the other individual's position. Then he resolutely uses the necessary semantically significant information to activate the mechanism that verbally induces a shift in the position of the other person. If the verbal inducement fails, the aggressive individual will look for other methods of circumventing the obstacle. One must be aggressive (without being in any way belligerent or dominating) because we live in an aggressive society.

The Input of information for maintaining a high output of aggressiveness is:

> *Because this is an aggressive society that I live in, it is necessary that I always have an aggressive attitude to life in general and towards the achievement of my goal[s] in particular.*
>
> *In every situation with which I am confronted, I am as aggressive as that situation demands.*

You may think that the habit of empathy is incompatible with the habit of aggressiveness but this is not so. Feeling empathy for another person does not mean that you must agree with the point of view he holds, merely that you have the ability to understand why he holds it. In cybernetic terms, it means that as the two of you cross-communicate your respective information, you have the acumen to recognize the Conceptual Storage in the biocomputer of the other person. Developing the habit of empathy is important. The achievement of your goal(s) will often depend on the cooperation you receive from others and one of the swiftest ways to antagonize people is to tell them bluntly that they are wrong about something. Being empathetic is not easy when another person's point of view is diametrically opposed to yours. However, it becomes easier if you remember that his biocomputer is also seeking a goal, even though he may not be aware of the fact. Quite often his immediate goal is to see if you respect his right to his own point of view. If he sees that you do, he establishes Conceptual Storage about you indicating to him that you think he is an important person.

The Input of information for increasing empathy is:

> *The projection of my personality is such that I know what the people I come into contact with are feeling within a few minutes of engaging in conversation with them. As a result of my increasing ability to empathize with people, I am more understanding with everyone with whom I come into contact.*

I have previously said that excessive impatience is an unproductive habit, but I must point out that the reverse is also true; that a person can be *too* patient. The old saying about patience being a virtue is correct only up to a certain point. To be habitually long-suffering, if you are not satisfied with the conditions of your work or personal relationships, is not particularly commendable. You can allow life to slip past you.

Given a choice, I would prefer to see a person being impatient to being too patient. When you are evaluating your Output, you must decide if one of the two characteristics is impeding your progress toward your goals. If your Output is a reasonable balance between the two, you need not Input this information:

> *I am a much more patient person.*

Alternatively;

> *Because I have been too tolerant and patient with the circumstances of my life, I now feel impatient with these circumstances.*

The habit of concentration is very clear as a concept, and this Input of information will improve and strengthen it:

> *I now concentrate deeply at all times that it is necessary for me to concentrate on any subject. No extraneous thoughts or external conditions of my environment interfere with my ability to give my undivided attention to the subject of my concentration.*

If you are casual about punctuality, both in your personal and business life, you must correct this and Input the following information:

> *I am a punctual person. If I say that I will be somewhere at a specific time, I make every effort to be there a few minutes before the time. If I say I will do something within a specific time, I make every effort to do so.*

Self-reliance is a habit which is entwined with confidence. The more confident a person becomes, the more self-reliant he or she becomes. Self-reliant people do not sit around bellyaching about their circumstances in life. They establish goals to change those circumstances. You are already self-reliant; you will become more so with this Input:

> *I am a self-reliant person; an independent, thinking person who is intent upon reaching the goal[s] I set myself. Because I am in control of my biocomputer, I can rely on myself to handle any situation with poise and with confidence.*

High on the list of desirable attributes in a dynamic society must be the habit of having an outgoing personality. To be sure that we both have the same Conceptual Storage relative to outgoing personality, it will help if I tell you that the opposite are people who are shy, or diffident. They are not comfortable when meeting new people and have difficulty expressing their ideas and opinions, even with friends. Intellectually they are often clever people, but they have the wrong program in their biocomputer—the wrong Permanent Storage.

There is no doubt that this storage became established in what can justifiably be called "the ten terrible years" from 2 to 12 years of age. Ask anyone who is shy how long this aspect of their personality has existed and invariably they will tell you that they have been this way as long as they can remember. If you have infants, I urge you to choose the words you use with them with as much care as is possible. One of the worst things that can be said to young children is "You should be seen and not heard." As a parent, you should never forget that one of the functions of the RAS is to accept or to reject Input. But the intellectual capacity to analyze the content of experiences does not start to develop until an individual has reached the age of about five, and even afterwards, the development is not that fast. This is why a child of six or seven can still believe that Santa Claus goes travelling over the roof tops on Christmas Eve. If you use the expression "You should be seen and not heard" to a ten or eleven year old, you are likely to receive a defiant "why not?" But a five year old may take it literally.

It is of the utmost importance that parents and teachers realize that when they say anything to a child under a certain age, it goes straight into the biocomputer. It is no exaggeration to say that "You should be seen and not heard," "You are stupid," and many other thought-less expressions used by way of admonition could have an effect on the individual to whom they are said for many years. They may be programmed into the biocom-puter and become *Permanent Storage.* Just as a mechani-cal computer is as good at a specific function as it is programmed to be, a human being is as good at living as he is educated to be.

Although they may not like to think of the matter in this way, the parent and the teacher are programming the youngster because it is they who are helping the child to establish the three kinds of storage—Word, Experiential, and Conceptual—without which the child would be un-able to integrate itself into society. Certainly there is a different program in every biocomputer, but the basic building blocks of the personality is the same in every biocomputer. In those early formative years the child has a mountain of information to process and take into stor-age. To do this, its RAS *has* to be in the deactivated state, without the ability to reject. Nowhere in the world is this better understood than in Russia. The Russian Commun-ists know that their regime is secure as long as they control the dissemination of information within the State and within the *educational system.* As a leading Soviet educator, Y. A. Gastev, put it to the Conference on Cyber-netics in Moscow in 1974: "It is quite natural to apply to the science concerned with teaching—a particular case of control—the ideas and methods of Cybernetics, the science dealing with control."

But the inability of very young children to reject certain kinds of Input need not be viewed simply as an invitation to propagandize them politically. On the contrary, it gives parents and teachers an unparalleled opportunity to ensure that their children will grow into strong, independent, self-confident adults. If you have young children, you will certainly want to teach them to say "please," "thank you," and "excuse me." But above all, you *must* encourage them to say and think, as often as possible, such life-enhancing things as "I'm smart," "I can do it," "I'm not afraid."

The Input of information for having a more outgoing personality is:

> *I now express my ideas, opinions, and feelings freely but tactfully. I enjoy meeting new people, and I meet them with ease and with comfort. I show the new people that I meet and the people that I know now that I am friendly and that I think they are important people. I praise others freely and sincerely.*

Do you think that creativity is limited to the Arts? People can be creative in many other ways. Salespeople must be creative in their prospecting, in the way they make presentations, and the way they arrange financing.

Do you remember Bob Porter's goal contract in Chapter 7? It is a good example of creativity. While doing his job as a fireman he is creating two professions for himself. Look at Jean Jackson's goal. Perhaps you cannot see anything creative about her goal but that would be because the Conceptual Storage in your biocomputer relative to creativity is too narrow. Jean is intent upon creating an ideal domestic environment where the entire family will be happier.

What could be more creative than that?

Do you think you are doing your work as creatively as is possible? By Inputting the following information, you will find that creative ideas are going to come to you

when you least expect them. Of course, the moment you
have put down your goal you have created something.

> *From this moment creative ideas come to me both
> when I want them and when I least expect them.
> They help me to increase my productivity. I imme-
> diately recognize these ideas and reward myself by
> converting the ideas into action that takes me more
> quickly to my goal[s].*

We all would do better if we spoke with more authority
and conviction. For example, the veteran sales professional can easily become blasé and lose business by
speaking with less authority and conviction than he did
earlier in his career. Because they lack Experiential Storage, it is to be expected that novices find it difficult to
speak with authority and conviction until they have
intimate knowledge of their product or service. This can
be quite difficult if they are not in the habit of processing
and storing information rapidly and efficiently. But this
is not only true of the sales professional, *it is true of
society as a whole.* As Alvin Toffler so brilliantly points
out in *Future Shock:*

> *As experience and scientific research pumps re-
> fined and accurate knowledge into society, new
> concepts, new ways of thinking, supersede, con-
> tradict and render obsolete older ideas and world
> views. Today change is so swift and relentless in
> the techno-societies that yesterday's truths sud-
> denly become today's fictions, and the most highly
> skilled and intelligent members of society admit
> difficulty in keeping up with the deluge of new
> knowledge—even in extremely narrow fields.*

It is for this reason that I want you to pay particular
attention to the Input of information into your biocompu-

ter for increasing your capacity to take into storage and *easily retrieve any new information.*

> *When I am engaged in a conversation or discussion with any one or a group of people, I speak with authority and conviction on those subjects with which I am fully acquainted. When I am reading, watching, listening to subjects about which it is necessary for me to acquire information and knowledge as a result of doing so with pleasure and interest, I have the ability to rapidly absorb all this information, and I have total and instant recall of that information and knowledge at any future time.*

In the field of self-improvement, I suppose more has been written and spoken about enthusiasm than most other human characteristics. I am sure that you have the intelligence to realize that you can accomplish little that is worthwhile without an enthusiastic approach to the achievement of your objectives and to life in general.

The Input of this information will ensure that you maintain a high level of enthusiasm. As you use this Word Storage when you are using RASCON, generate within yourself the feeling of enthusiasm that you have when you are engaged in a very pleasurable pursuit:

> *At this very moment I feel wonderfully enthusiatic about my life and my work, and I now act in a very enthusiastic manner. I know that enthusiasm is contagious, and that as I continue to feel and act in an enthusiastic manner, other people will catch my spirit of enthusiasm.*

When you have used RASCON a minimum of forty-two times you will be ready to shorten the systematic relaxation to something between 1 to 2 minutes. This is the shortened monologue you will now use.

> *I am thinking of my legs and I'm allowing my legs to relax.*
>
> *I have allowed both of my legs to become so relaxed that my legs are now feeling very limp and heavy.*
>
> *I have allowed both of my legs to become so relaxed that my legs are now feeling very limp and heavy.*
>
> *Now I will allow all of the muscles in the front of my body to relax.*
>
> *I'm breathing deeply and rhythmically, and with each rhythmic breath I take, I become more and more pleasantly relaxed.*
>
> *Relaxation spreads around to my back, and I'm allowing all the muscles in my back to relax.*
>
> *Relaxation continues up my spine through my central nervous system, relaxing muscle and tissue and sinew all over my body.*
>
> *Now I will allow my shoulders to relax. I've allowed my shoulders to become so relaxed that my shoulders are drooping and sagging.*
>
> *My arms are hanging from my shoulders, and as my arms become more relaxed, my arms feel very limp and heavy.*
>
> *I have allowed all of my facial muscles to relax.*
>
> *I've allowed the smallest muscles in my body— the muscles around my eyelids—to relax, and my eyelids feel very heavy. I slip gently into a deep state of complete and utter relaxation.*

Input all the information as you have the previous forty-two times and add to that this additional information:

> *Because this is an aggressive society that I live in,*

it is necessary that I always have an aggressive attitude to life in general and toward the achievement of my goal[s] in particular. In every situation with which I am confronted, I am as aggressive as that situation demands.

The projection of my personality is such that I know what the people I come into contact with are feeling within a few minutes of engaging in conversation with them. As a result of my increasing ability to empathize with people, I am more understanding with everyone with whom I come into contact. I am a much more patient person.

Alternatively;

Because I have been too tolerant and patient with the circumstances of my life, I now feel impatient with these circumstances.

I now concentrate deeply at all times that it is necessary for me to concentrate on any subject. No extraneous thoughts or external conditions of my environment interfere with my ability to give my undivided attention to the subject of my concentration.

I am a punctual person. If I say that I will be somewhere at a specific time, I make every effort to be there a few minutes before the time. If I say I will do something within a specific time, I make every effort to do so.

I am a self-reliant person; an independent, thinking person who is intent upon reaching the goal[s] I set myself. Because I am in control of my biocomputer, I can rely on myself to handle any situation with poise and with confidence.

I now express my ideas, opinions, and feelings freely but tactfully. I enjoy meeting new people, and I meet them with ease and with comfort. I show the new people that I meet and the people that I know now that I am friendly and that I think they are important people. I praise others freely and sincerely.

From this moment, creative ideas come to me both when I want them and when I least expect them which will help me to increase my productivity. I immediately recognize these ideas and reward myself by converting the ideas into action which will take me more quickly to my goal[s].

When I am engaged in a conversation or discussion with any one or a group of people, I speak with authority and conviction on those subjects with which I am fully acquainted. When I am reading, watching, listening to subjects about which it is necessary for me to acquire information and knowledge as a result of doing so with pleasure and interest, I have the ability to rapidly absorb all this information and I have total and instant recall of that information and knowledge at any future time.

At this very moment, I feel wonderfully enthusiastic about my life and my work and I now act in a very enthusiastic manner. I know that enthusiasm is contagious and that as I continue to feel and act in an enthusiastic manner, other people will catch my spirit of enthusiasm.

Spend the amount of time you have become accustomed to spending using Psychofeedback.

Stop using RASCON.

When you have used RASCON a minimum of fifty-six times you will be ready to do the fourth and final exercise. It is much more difficult than those you have already done so do not be overly concerned if you have difficulty with it. The people who experience some difficulty do so because they either take longer to get their imaginations working subjectively or they have not taken a sufficient amount of time to go through the systematic relaxation. There is a direct correlation between the length of time spent on the systematic relaxation and the degree of deactivation of the RAS in the early stages of learning how to use RASCON. If you find you are unable to do the arm exercise, try it again after taking 3 to 4 minutes on the systematic relaxation instead of the 1 to 2 minutes you have been taking these past fourteen times.

When you have taken the 1 to 2 minutes on the systematic relaxation, then raise your right arm straight out from your shoulder at shoulder level, with the palm of your hand facing downward and with your fingers outstretched. Imagine as vividly as you can that your arm is carved from one piece of wood, using these words:

> *My arm is carved from one piece of wood and my arm is becoming very stiff and rigid. My arm is carved from one piece of wood and my arm is becoming very stiff and rigid. Very stiff and rigid. Very stiff and rigid. My arm is now carved from one piece of wood, and it is impossible for me to bend my arm. It will be impossible for me to bend my arm until I touch it with my left hand. I will try to bend my arm, but the harder I try, the more stiff and rigid it becomes.*

You must use these words with some intensity, emphasizing the semantically significant words *stiff* and *rigid*. When you say, "I will try to bend my arm, but the harder I try, the more stiff and rigid it becomes," then try to bend your arm. You will find that, try as hard as you may, you are unable to bend your arm until you touch it with the opposite hand.

There may be some doubt on your part as to whether or not you have actually been able to do this exercise. This is very natural considering the number of years which have passed without your realizing that you had this power within you.

It is, of course, another giant step that you have

taken in the control you have established over your bio-computer. Because it is so contrary to our most commonly held belief about the degree of control we are capable of exercising over ourselves, doubt is the most natural reaction to this self-discovery. That was exactly the reaction shown by those individuals who had to learn to use electrical apparatus for the implementation of therapeutic biofeedback. They do have an advantage over you, inso-far as being in the position of observing, externally, the measure of control they are achieving over their internal mechanisms. While it is not always necessarily so, in this instance, seeing is most definitely believing, and there is no room for doubt as what they have accomplished.

But it is important that you understand that it did not matter whether, initially, they believed or did not believe, providing they understood what they had to do and did exactly as they were instructed. The same is true of the course of instruction contained in this book.

It is frequently said that in order to achieve their potential, people must eliminate all doubts about their ability. However, if the goal(s) you set for yourself is/are very high, it is not possible to prevent some doubt from surfacing, particularly when you experience setbacks. But that does not matter, providing that kind of thinking is not the dominant Input of information into the biocom-puter and, with the correct use of willpower, these thoughts are kept in control and minimized.

Having used RASCON a mimimum of fifty-six times, you are now ready to shorten the systematic relax-ation to a few seconds, i.e., the length of time it takes you to say to yourself silently and meaningfully: Four, my legs are relaxed. Three, my torso is relaxed. Two, my shoulders and arms are relaxed. One, my entire body is relaxed.

You are now at the end of the beginning. The most important part of the program lies *in the months and years ahead of you.*

By doing all the things I have asked of you, you have established the "thought formula" as Permanent Storage in your biocomputer. *It will remain as* Permanent Storage *only* if you maintain it as such, by the activity across the synaptic gaps of all the neuron chains concerned with the words, phrases, and sentences contained within the "thought formula."

Read again the explanation of how Circulating Storage becomes Permanent Storage because each time you read the words, and process the information, it will become more meaningful to you.

At least once every week, use RASCON exclusively for the purpose of maintaining and consolidating the "thought formula" as Permanent Storage. If you do so, it will attract similar storage.

Why do I want you to be in a position to use RASCON in seconds? Very simply, the reason is because I want you to start looking for ways to put RASCON to work. I mean ways other than using Psychofeedback and maintaining the correct Permanent Storage in your biocomputer.

For example, if you are a salesperson, you know that the only way you will make sales is to make calls, so use RASCON to combat call reluctance. In other words, *don't let it happen*. Suppose you have decided to do some prospecting on the telephone. Pause for just one minute, sitting at your desk, use RASCON and Input this or similar information:

"In a moment I am going to make phone calls. I will enjoy every call I make. If my prospect does not require my services this will not disturb me in any way but will only make me more eager to get on with the next call. I feel supremely confident in myself and my ability."

Similarly, use RASCON before you make a sales presentation. Suppose you have an appointment to make a sales presentation, it does not matter where you have the appointment, it could be in a home, or somebody's

office or your own office. Wherever it is, you should allow
yourself enough time, so that, before meeting your pro-
spective customer, you use RASCON and Input the correct information for your biocomputer to act upon,
similar to the following:

"In a few minutes I will meet John Doe. I feel
supremely confident in myself. I will speak with authority and conviction. All the information related to my
product will come easily to my tongue. I will recognize
any objection and deal with it efficiently and tactfully
before it can be of consequence. When the moment comes
for me to close my sale, I will close at that moment and
ask for the order. I enjoy selling and I look forward with
pleasure to my meeting."

Please do not think that this short period of time is
wasted. It could be the most important part of the entire
presentation.

Another example. I use RASCON extensively for
problem solving. When I have a problem and use RAS-
CON, I think about the problem to the exclusion of all
else. I feed into my biocomputer all the facts related to the
problem. I include the imponderables—those elements
which may not be directly and factually related to the
problem and yet have some bearing on it. Depending on
the complexity of the problem, I may spend anything
from three to ten minutes in a state of complete and utter
relaxation while I demand an answer to the problem.
When I have switched off RASCON, *I do not think of the
problem again* because I trust my biocomputer. It has
never let me down.

How often have you been faced with a troublesome
problem and have said that you are "going to sleep on it"
with the result that, having done so, the problem appears
to resolve itself. When you stopped bombarding your
biocomputer with useless information, it set about the
task of finding the answer to the problem.

You already trust your biocomputer in so many

ways. When you drive the lethal weapon you call an automobile, how many times do you think death brushes past you by only a matter of inches? Do not deceive yourself with the notion that you drive your car with your mind. It is mentally impossible for you to work out how to lift your foot off the throttle and onto the brake. In this instance, a matter of your life or death, you trust your biocomputer implicitly.

When you learn to trust it in the same manner with other, no less critical aspects of your life, it will perform magnificently for you. And you, in turn, will begin to perform magnificently because of it.

Appendix: Behavior, Purpose, and Teleology

by Arturo Rosenblueth, Norbert Wiener,
and Julian Bigelow

This essay has two goals. The first is to define the behavioristic study of natural events and to classify behavior. The second is to stress the importance of the concept of purpose.

Given any object, relatively abstracted from its surroundings for study, the behavioristic approach consists in the examination of the output of the object and of the relations of this output to the input. By output is meant any change produced in the surroundings by the object. By input, conversely, is meant any event external to the object that modifies this object in any manner.

The above statement of what is meant by the behavioristic method of study omits the specific structure and the intrinsic organization of the object. This omission is fundamental because on it is based the distinction between the behavioristic and the alternative functional method of study. In a functional analysis, as opposed to a behavioristic approach, the main goal is the intrinsic organization of the entity studied, its structure and its properties; the relations between the object and the surroundings are relatively incidental.

From this definition of the behavioristic method a broad definition of behavior ensues. By behavior is meant any change of an entity with respect to its surroundings. This change may be largely an output from the object, the input being then minimal, remote or irrelevant; or else the change may be immediately traceable to a certain input. Accordingly, any modification of an object, detectable externally, may be denoted as behavior. The term would be, therefore, too extensive for usefulness were it not that it may be restricted by apposite adjectives—i.e., that behavior may be classified.

The consideration of the changes of energy involved in behavior affords a basis for classification. Active behavior is that in which the object is the source of the output energy involved in a given specific reaction. The object may store energy supplied by a remote or relatively immediate input, but the input does not energize the output directly. In passive behavior, on the contrary, the object is not a source of energy; all the energy in the output can be traced to the immediate input (e.g., the throwing of an object), or else the object may control energy which remains external to it throughout the reaction (e.g., the soaring flight of a bird).

Active behavior may be subdivided into two classes; purposeless (or random) and purposeful. The term purposeful is meant to denote that the act or behavior may be interpreted as directed to the attainment of a goal—i.e., to a final condition in which the behaving object reaches a definite correlation in time or in space with respect to another object or event. Purposeless behavior then is that which is not interpreted as directed to a goal.

The vagueness of the words "may be interpreted"

as used above might be considered so great that the distinction would be useless. Yet the recognition that behavior may sometimes be purposeful is unavoidable and useful, as follows. The basis of the concept of purpose is the awareness of "voluntary activity." Now, the purpose of voluntary acts is not a matter of arbitrary interpretation but a physiological fact. When we perform a voluntary action what we select voluntarily is a specific purpose, not a specific movement. Thus, if we decide to take a glass containing water and carry it to our mouth we do not command certain muscles to contract to a certain degree and in a certain sequence; we merely trip the purpose and the reaction follows automatically. Indeed, experimental physiology has so far been largely incapable of explaining the mechanism of voluntary activity. We submit that this failure is due to the fact that when an experimenter stimulates the motor regions of the cerebral cortex he does not duplicate a voluntary reaction; he trips efferent, "output" pathways, but does not trip a purpose, as is done voluntarily.

The view has often been expressed that all machines are purposeful. This view is untenable. First may be mentioned mechanical devices such as roulette, designed precisely for purposelessness. Then may be considered devices such as a clock, designed, it is true, with a purpose, but having a performance which, although orderly, is not purposeful—i.e., there is no specific final condition toward which the movement of the clock strives. Similarly, although a gun may be used for a definite purpose, the attainment of a goal is not intrinsic to the performance of the gun; random shooting can be made, deliberately purposeless.

Some machines, on the other hand, are intrinsically purposeful. A torpedo with a target-seeking mechanism is an example. The term servomechanisms has been coined precisely to designate machines with intrinsic purposeful behavior.

It is apparent from these considerations that although the definition of purposeful behavior is relatively vague, and hence operationally largely meaningless, the concept of purpose is useful and should, therefore, be retained.

Purposeful active behavior may be subdivided into two classes: "feed-back" (or "teleological") and "non-feed-back" (or "non-teleological"). The expression feed-back is used by engineers in two different senses. In a broad sense it may denote that some of the output energy of an apparatus or machine is returned as input; an example is an electrical amplifier with feed-back. The feed-back is in these cases positive—the fraction of the output which reenters the object has the same sign as the original input signal. Positive feed-back adds to the input signals, it does not correct them. The term feed-back is also employed in a more restricted sense to signify that the behavior of an object is controlled by the margin of error at which the object stands at a given time with reference to a relatively specific goal. The feed-back is then negative, that is, the signals from the goal are used to restrict outputs which would otherwise go beyond the goal. It is this second meaning of the term feed-back that is used here.

All purposeful behavior may be considered to require negative feed-back. If a goal is to be attained, some signals from the goal are necessary at some time to direct the behavior. By non-feed-back behavior is meant that in which there are no signals from the goal which modify the activity of the object in the course of behavior. Thus, a machine may be set to impinge upon a luminous object although the machine may be insensitive to light. Similarly, a snake may strike at a frog, or a frog at a fly, with no visual or other report from the prey after the movement has started. Indeed, the movement is in these cases so fast that it is not likely that nerve impulses would have time to arise at the retina, travel to the central nervous system and set up further impulses which would reach the muscles in time to modify the movement effectively.

As opposed to the examples considered, the behavior of some machines and some reactions of living organisms involve a continuous feed-back from the goal that modifies and guides the behaving object. This type of behavior is more effective than that mentioned above, particularly when the goal is not stationary. But continuous feed-back control may lead to very clumsy behavior if the feed-back is inadequately damped and becomes therefore positive instead of negative for certain frequencies of oscillation. Suppose, for example, that a machine is designed with the purpose of impinging upon a moving luminous goal; the path followed by the machine is controlled by the direction and intensity of the light from the goal. Suppose further that the machine overshoots seriously when it follows a movement of the goal in a certain direction; an even stronger stimulus will then be delivered which will turn the machine in the opposite direction. If that movement again overshoots, a series of increasingly larger oscillations will ensue and the machine will miss the goal.

This picture of the consequences of undamped feed-back is strikingly similar to that seen during the performance of a voluntary act by a cerebellar patient. At rest the subject exhibits no obvious motor disturbance. If he is asked to carry a glass of water from a table to his mouth, however, the hand carrying the glass will execute a series of oscillatory motions of increasing amplitude as the glass approaches his mouth, so that the water will spill and the purpose will not be fulfilled. This test is typical of the disorderly motor performance of patients with cerebellar disease. The analogy with the behavior of a machine with undamped feed-back is so vivid that we venture to suggest that the main function of the cerebellum is the control of the feed-back nervous mechanisms involved in purposeful motor activity.

Feed-back purposeful behavior may again be subdivided. It may be extrapolative (predictive), or it may be non-extrapolative (non-predictive). The reactions of unicellular organisms known as tropisms are examples of non-preductive performances. The amoeba merely follows the source to which it reacts; there is no evidence that it extrapolates the path of a moving source. Predictive animal behavior, on the other hand, is a commonplace. A cat starting to pursue a running mouse does not run directly toward the region where the mouse is at any given time, but moves toward an extrapolated future position. Examples of both predictive and non-predictive servomechanisms may also be found readily.

Predictive behavior may be subdivided into different orders. The cat chasing the mouse is an instance of first-order prediction; the cat merely predicts the path of the mouse. Throwing a stone at a moving target requires a second-order prediction; the paths of the target and of the stone should be foreseen. Examples of predictions of higher order are shooting with a sling or with a bow and arrow.

Predictive behavior requires the discrimination of at least two coordinates, a temporal and at least one spatial axis. Prediction will be more effective and flexible, however, if the behaving object can respond to changes in more than one spatial coordinate. The sensory receptors of an organism, or the corresponding elements of a machine, may therefore limit the predictive behavior. Thus, a bloodhound follows a trail, that is, it does not show any predictive behavior in trailing, because a chemical, olfactory input reports only spatial information: distance, as indicated by intensity. The external changes capable of affecting auditory, or, even better, visual receptors, permit more accurate spatial localization; hence the possibility of more effective predictive reactions when the input affects those receptors.

In addition to the limitations imposed by the receptors upon the ability to perform extrapolative actions, limitations may also occur that are due to the internal organization of the behaving object. Thus, a machine which is to trail predictively a moving luminous object should not only be sensitive to light (e.g., by the possession of a photoelectric cell), but should also have the structure adequate for interpreting the luminous input. It is probable that limitations of internal organization, particularly of the organization of the central nervous system, determine the complexity of predictive behavior which a mammal may attain. Thus, it is likely that the nervous system of a rat or dog is such that it does not permit the integration of input and output necessary for the performance of a predictive reaction of the third or fourth order. Indeed, it is possible that one of the features of the discontinuity of behavior observable when comparing humans with other high mammals may lie in that the other mammals are limited to predictive behavior of a low order, whereas man may be capable potentially of quite high orders of prediction.

The classification of behavior suggested so far is tabulated here:

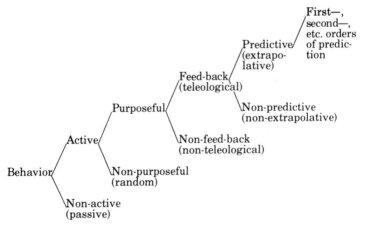

It is apparent that each of the dichotomies established singles out arbitrarily one feature, deemed interesting, leaving an amorphous remainder: the non-class. It is also apparent that the criteria for the several dichotomies are heterogeneous. It is obvious, therefore, that many other lines of classification are available, which are independent of that developed above. Thus, behavior in general, or any of the groups in the table, could be divided into linear (i.e., output proportional to input) and non-linear. A division into continuous and discontinuous might be useful for many purposes. The several degrees of freedom which behavior may exhibit could also be employed as a basis of systematization.

The classification tabulated above was adopted for several reasons. It leads to the singling out of the class of predictive behavior, a class particularly interesting since it suggests the possibility of systematizing increasingly more complex tests of the behavior of organisms. It emphasizes the concepts of purpose and of teleology, concepts which, although rather discredited at present, are shown to be important. Finally, it reveals that a uniform behavioristic analysis is applicable to both machines and living organisms, regardless of the complexity of the behavior.

It has sometimes been stated that the designers of machines merely attempt to duplicate the performances of living organisms. This statement is uncritical. That the gross behavior of some machines should be similar to the reactions of organisms is not surprising. Animal behavior includes many varieties of all the possible modes of behavior and the machines devised so far have far from exhausted all those possible modes. There is, therefore, a considerable overlap of the two realms of behavior. Examples, however, are readily found of man-made machines with behavior that transcends human behavior. A machine with an electrical output is an instance; for men, unlike the electric fishes, are incapable of emitting electricity. Radio transmission is perhaps an even better instance, for no animal is known with the ability to generate short waves, even if so-called experiments on telepathy are considered seriously.

A further comparison of living organisms and machines leads to the following inferences. The methods of study for the two groups are at present similar. Whether they should always be the same may depend on whether or not there are one or more qualitatively distinct, unique characteristics present in one group and absent in the other. Such qualitative differences have not appeared so far.

The broad classes of behavior are the same in machines and in living organisms. Specific, narrow classes may be found exclusively in one or the other. Thus, no machine is available yet that can write a Sanscrit-Mandarin dictionary. Thus, also, no living organism is known that rolls on wheels—imagine what the result would have been if engineers had insisted on copying living organisms and had therefore put legs and feet in their locomotives, instead of wheels.

While the behavioristic analysis of machines and living organisms is largely uniform, their functional study reveals deep differences. Structurally, organisms are mainly colloidal, and include prominently protein molecules, large, complex and anisotropic; machines are chiefly metallic and include mainly simple molecules. From the standpoint of their energetics, machines usually exhibit relatively large differences of potential, which permit rapid mobilization of energy; in organisms the emerge is more uniformly distributed, it is not very mobile. Thus, in electric machines conduction is mainly electronic, whereas in organisms electric changes are usually ionic.

Scope and flexibility are achieved in machines largely by temporal multiplication of effects; frequencies of one million per second or more are readily obtained and utilized. In organisms, spatial multiplication, rather than temporal, is the rule; the temporal achievements are poor—the fastest nerve fibers can only conduct about one thousand impulses per second; spatial multiplication is on the other hand abundant and admirable in its compactness. This difference is well illustrated by the comparison of a television receiver and the eye. The television receiver may be described as a single cone retina; the images are formed by scanning—i.e., by orderly successive detection of the signal with a rate of about 20 million per second. Scanning is a process which seldom or never occurs in organisms, since it requires fast frequencies for effective performance. The eye uses a spatial, rather than a temporal multiplier. Instead of the one cone of the television receiver a human eye has about 6.5 million cones and about 115 million rods.

If an engineer were to design a robot, roughly similar in behavior to an animal organism, he would not attempt at present to make it out of proteins and other colloids. He would probably build it out of metallic parts, some dielectrics and many vacuum tubes. The movements of the robot could readily be much faster and more powerful than those of the original organism. Learning and memory, however, would be quite rudimentary. In future years, as the knowledge of colloids and proteins increases, future engineers may attempt the design of robots not only with a behavior, but also with a structure similar to that of a mammal. The ultimate model of a cat is of course another cat, whether it be born of still another cat or synthesized in a laboratory.

In classifying behavior the term "teleology" was used as synonymous with "purpose controlled by feedback." Teleology has been interpreted in the past to imply purpose and the vague concept of a "final cause" has been often added. This concept of final causes has led to the opposition of teleology to determinism. A discussion of causality, determinism, and final causes is beyond the scope of this essay. It may be pointed out, however, that purposefulness, as defined here, is quite independent of causality, initial or final. Teleology has been discredited chiefly because it was defined to imply a cause subsequent in time to a given effect. When this aspect of teleology was dismissed, however, the associated recognition of the importance of purpose was also unfortunately discarded. Since we consider purposefulness a concept necessary for the understanding of certain modes of behavior we suggest that a teleological study is useful if it avoids problems of causality and concerns itself merely with an investigation of purpose.

We have restricted the connotation of teleological behavior by applying this designation only to purposeful reactions which are controlled by the error of the reaction—i.e., by the difference between the state of the behaving object at any time and the final state interpreted as the purpose. Teleological behavior thus becomes synonymous with behavior controlled by negative feed-back, and gains therefore in precision by a sufficiently restricted connotation.

According to this limited definition, teleology is not opposed to determinism, but to non-teleology. Both teleological and non-teleological systems are deterministic when the behavior considered belongs to the realm where determinism applies. The concept of teleology shares only one thing with the concept of causality: a time axis. But causality implies a one-way, relatively irreversible functional relationship, whereas teleology is concerned with behavior, not with functional relationships.